HAC
DISCIPLINE TOGETHER

"*Hacking School Discipline Together* acknowledges the very real demands teachers and administrators face when dealing with discipline and offers practical and doable solutions that can be implemented immediately and systemically. Benson also takes time to address common areas of push-back respectfully and logically, helping administrators make the case for building a *status quo* of restoration instead of a culture of punishment."

— **ROBYN JACKSON,** AUTHOR OF NINE BOOKS, INCLUDING THE BESTSELLING *NEVER WORK HARDER THAN YOUR STUDENTS* AND THE AWARD-WINNING *NEVER UNDERESTIMATE YOUR TEACHERS*

"This is the missing manual for responsive discipline practices. Benson reminds us that we need a 'well-constructed and integrated system' of disciplinary responses. Too many schools think it's enough to do restorative circles when they really need a rich and diverse toolkit for helping teachers and students restore harmony and repair harm. Benson invites us to expand our repertoire and level up our game."

— **ZARETTA HAMMOND,** AUTHOR OF *CULTURALLY RESPONSIVE TEACHING AND THE BRAIN*

"Veteran educator Jeffrey Benson draws from a career of more than forty years as a teacher and administrator to offer sage and practical advice for dealing with disruptive student behaviors. His book is unique in that it goes beyond describing specific discipline strategies for individuals to offer a blueprint for collective action via a systemic, schoolwide approach to handling infractions with consistency and empathy. You could spend thirty or forty years acquiring the wisdom he offers ... or you could read this valuable book."

— **JAY McTIGHE,** EDUCATION CONSULTANT AND COAUTHOR OF ELEVEN BOOKS, INCLUDING THE INTERNATIONAL BESTSELLER *UNDERSTANDING BY DESIGN*

"They say that storytelling is data with a soul, and Jeffrey Benson is truly a master storyteller. Sit back and enjoy learning how a school shifted from a culture of frustration and stress to an environment of power, respect, and cooperation for both students and faculty. You'll love all the practical tools he provides as he relates these real-life experiences."

— **MARGARET SEARLE,** ACADEMIC AND BEHAVIOR CONSULTANT AND AUTHOR

"Jeffrey Benson writes, 'We get accustomed to dysfunction,' and he's right. That's human nature (and a survival skill). But he also believes that thoughtful attitudes and systems can improve student behavior. His book *Hacking School Discipline Together* is a treasure trove of practical ideas and strategies to help students learn and work as productive members of the community. His What You Can Do Tomorrow sections, for example, provide realistic and reasonable strategies for addressing difficult situations and implementing them right away. This book is a terrific tool for faculty conversations and collegiality."

— **TOM HOERR,** SCHOOL LEADER AND AUTHOR OF *THE FORMATIVE FIVE*

"Jeffrey Benson is a fabulous go-to author when it comes to encouraging and informing administrators, teachers, and all staff members. He's written an easy-to-read, *well*-thought-out book for both new and veteran educators who want to be more strategic and thoughtful when handling student discipline. *Hacking School Discipline Together* is a must-read for creating systems and structures to support all students."

— **JENNIFER ABRAMS,** EDUCATIONAL CONSULTANT AND AUTHOR OF *HAVING HARD CONVERSATIONS*

"How much time and energy are expended in schools every day dealing with discipline issues? Too often, schools don't have systems and structures that provide fair and consistent support for kids who struggle with behavior. And, without clear systems, the adults involved become dysregulated right along with the kids. Thank you, Jeffrey Benson, for offering practical and wise guidance for educators to help adults and kids navigate these tricky waters. This book is a much-needed resource!"

— **MIKE ANDERSON,** AUTHOR OF *TACKLING THE MOTIVATION CRISIS*

HACKING SCHOOL DISCIPLINE TOGETHER

ALL NEW CONTENT

10 Ways to Create a Culture of Empathy and Responsibility Using **Schoolwide** Restorative Justice

HACK™ Learning SERIES

JEFFREY BENSON

Hacking School Discipline Together

Highland Heights, OH 44143 USA
Website: 10publications.com

Cover and Interior Design by Steven Plummer
Editing by Tarah Threadgill
Copyediting by Jennifer Jas
Project Management by Regina Bell

Paperback ISBN: 978-1-956512-50-2
Hardcover ISBN: 978-1-956512-51-9
eBook ISBN: 978-1-956512-52-6

Library of Congress Cataloging-in-Publication Data is available for this title.

First Printing: January 2024

TABLE OF CONTENTS

PREFACE

"C" WAS THE first of my many students whose struggles kept me up at night. I oversaw the resource room for students who were frustrated, sad, or falling behind in their work. As was the case with most of my crew, C didn't fit into the often-regimented and inflexible school environment. He was consistently in trouble, not so much for the rules he had broken—which were of the misdemeanor kind, such as yelling or moaning loudly in frustration—but for his reactions to the adults who told him to stop. He often loudly complained that he was behaving no worse than anyone else, asserting that he would not be showing up for detention and telling the adults that, no matter what they said, he didn't care.

I was at the beginning of my career, and I had a small toolkit of strategies. Mostly, I knew I was being paid to hang in with C when everyone else had given up. That was hard work; I, too, did not like to be told by C that he didn't care about anything I said. I always seemed a few steps behind whatever was triggering his frustration. All those hours I spent awake at night, trying to predict his reactions to my plans for the next day, yielded so few useful ideas. I would have been better off with a good night's sleep.

One day, after a difficult interaction with C, I said to him, "I wish I knew how to help you more. I wish I knew what I could have done." He said, "Well, yeah," and smiled at me.

Out of honesty and with no greater skills, we repeated that short dialogue many a time. I believe that's what gave me traction in earning his trust. Occasionally, he would express to me regrets for his outbursts aimed at other adults in the school. He reluctantly did go to detentions, which deepened his sense of dread for his future. The school had no restorative practices. Sometimes, I sent a note to the main office that C would serve his detentions with me. He would quietly straighten the bookshelves or sweep the room—and then he would ask me to give him another chore. He was straining against the system to be made whole by contributing positively to the school in a way equal to his transgressions. He wanted to even the score, if only in my eyes.

Now, I see his occasional posts on social media, and I know that C has gone on to have a family and a place in his community. The time we worked together was the seed that took almost fifty years to grow into this book. That's why I've dedicated this book to C and other students who long for us to help them be whole again.

INTRODUCTION

BUILD SKILLS, ACCOUNTABILITY, AND RELATIONSHIPS

Most of the big problems we encounter in organizations or society are ambiguous and evolving ... To solve [these] bigger, more ambiguous problems, we need to encourage open minds, creativity, and hope.

— Chip and Dan Heath, organizational theorists and authors

Schools live at the intersection of infinite demands and finite resources, a classic setup for conflict among those trying to get all their work done. As a nation, we have never funded, resourced, and staffed our schools to address the needs of all our students, many of them overwhelmed by the expectations, assumptions, and pace of their day. It's no surprise, therefore, when many students cope by misbehaving.

Those expectations, assumptions, and the pace of the day weigh on teachers, counselors, teaching assistants, nurses, and administrators. Addressing inevitable student misbehaviors will always interrupt somebody's work. The misbehaving student has, in essence, transgressed twice: first with their misbehavior and second by interrupting the adult who assumes responsibility for handling the situation with the student. Most school staff wish they better understood where their own responsibilities begin and end in response to student misbehavior (i.e., "Is this my job now?").

Without a well-constructed and integrated system of responses, we often reach for the quickest intervention, one that we hope will have the strongest impact on the student. Historically and currently, the primary tools are detentions, loss of privileges, and school suspensions. We threaten punishments, hoping that students will feel the pain of shaming, isolation, and exclusion enough to convince them to rein in their behavior. Such traditional punishment does work with some students who already have a toolkit of better behaviors and who have a strong affiliation with the adults, the culture, and the goals of the school.

But punishment does not build skills, improve relationships, or reinforce motivation for most students. When faced with a direct punishment for their actions, students reasonably conclude that their biggest mistake was getting caught. We can do better.

We can respond to student misbehavior with schoolwide structures and strategies in ways that allow them to be accountable, give back to the community, build their toolkit of coping under stress, increase trust in the adults who hold them accountable, and help them develop an internal drive to do the right thing. We can do so while decreasing simmering conflicts among staff when everyone has limited patience to handle another case of student misbehavior without knowing who, if anyone, will effectively step in. With predictable and flexible structures for handling all levels of misbehavior, the staff will operate in a culture that balances rules with autonomy.

A well-constructed system of responses to student misbehavior dovetails with the work being done to improve equity in our schools. Equity doesn't mean treating everyone exactly the same; it means developing the infrastructure to provide each student with what they need to learn. To do so, adults need a large and differentiated menu of responses to student misbehavior, just as they do a variety of pedagogical methods when students fail to understand a lesson.

A handful of teachers may stubbornly abide by the notion of "Spare the rod; spoil the child," fearing that a loss of a one-size-fits-all culture of punishment will lead to chaos. However, the data on repeated detentions, suspensions, and students dropping out—especially when we cast a light on the experiences of minority students—suggest that punishment doesn't work well enough. Punishment doesn't teach new skills and doesn't pull the student closer to the community. Punishment often replicates the inequities that plague our nation rather than heals them. If you still want strong measures, you will see later in this book that detentions and suspensions remain on the menu of adult responses, but only when those extreme measures are absolutely necessary.

Instead of reactively reaching for traditional punishment, we can build a school culture of responding to student misbehavior in a way that leverages what most of our teachers desire: better relationships with all students and a clearer understanding of what is expected from administration when students misbehave. This book provides a systematic pathway to reaching those goals.

I would be remiss not to note that a significant amount of student misbehavior could be eliminated if the standard curriculum were more developmentally appropriate and less overdriven by high-stakes testing. We could reduce student misbehavior with smaller classes, more access to the outdoors and community resources, and a greater integration of the arts and physical activity into the daily schedule. We could reduce student misbehavior with more attention to the executive functioning needs of students (especially adolescents) and more mental health professionals to ameliorate the impacts of poverty and injustice, which are the roots of so much trauma that shadows too many students.

But that's not the environment now in which our students and school staff work. In the meantime, we need to be compassionately ready for inevitable student misbehaviors. We need all teachers and administrators to be on the same page. We need to systemically hack school discipline.

The initial book in this series, *Hacking School Discipline* (Maynard and Weinstein, 2019), provided readers with a plethora of strategies that support strong student-teacher relationships and help us move away from a culture of punishment. Since the publication of that book, readers have asked for more in-depth information on how to apply these Hacks to an entire school in addition to individual classrooms. Maynard and Weinstein noted, "Policies that address the entire school often miss individual students and cases."

That's where this sequel, *Hacking School Discipline Together*, takes up, sharing more best practices for working with individual students and classes, this time within a school that is transforming its structures, protocols, and support systems to address misbehaviors. There is a pathway for teachers and administrators to work together, decreasing the tensions and conflicts when everyone seems to be going their own way in dealing with student misbehaviors. *Hacking School Discipline Together* provides that vision and the roadmap to get there.

HOW THIS BOOK IS ORGANIZED

In organizing the Hacks, I used the standard Hack Learning Series template. Each Hack is divided into seven sections:

- **The Problem:** A description of a common dilemma educators encounter in responding to student misbehavior.
- **The Hack:** A reframing of the problem to hack an entire school culture of discipline.
- **What You Can Do Tomorrow:** Specific actions for administrators and for staff that can be implemented immediately.

- **A Blueprint for Full Implementation:** Hacking school discipline requires confronting and changing long-held beliefs and practices. The recommendations in this section apply to administrators and staff working collaboratively, each within their own domains over a period of months, to implement effective schoolwide discipline practices that sustain over time.
- **Overcoming Pushback:** Pushback is not simply an impulsive resistance to change. Often, staff need more information and support to feel competent to do their part. This section addresses many common concerns staff have when a school seeks to change how they discipline misbehaving students.
- **The Hack in Action:** This section contains a story unfolding from Hack to Hack, as a fictional school with a recurring set of characters builds a discipline process that is predictable and flexible, where student misbehavior leads to teaching and inclusion. While the story must be classified as fiction, the events and characters are based on my work in many schools. The characters are amalgams of real administrators and staff members who worked to improve their responses to student misbehaviors in their schools. Each of those schools implemented the Hacks in an idiosyncratic fashion as we assessed the readiness and capacity of the school to successfully move forward. The story unfolding in The Hack in Action sections represents a recommended path to success.

I am indebted to all the hardworking and visionary educators who have traveled this path with me and have helped shape our stories and guidance into this book.

HACK 1

ESTABLISH EXPECTATIONS

DECIDE WHEN AN ADMINISTRATOR STEPS IN

Way I see it, everyone plays their own role in the world, and no role is more important than the other.

— Burna Boy, singer and songwriter

THE PROBLEM: STAFF DON'T KNOW WHEN ADMINISTRATORS SHOULD STEP IN

Nearly every adult who works in a school enters the building before the students arrive in the morning, each with a plan for the day. Teachers have their lessons ready; administrators have time set aside for essential meetings, working on the budget, or interviewing potential new staff; counselors and nurses have planned times for appointments, testing, and data entry into the system. And then, the school doors officially open for the day, with students flooding the hallways and filling the classrooms with all their energy and relationships, traumas and hopes. Rarely will a day in school go exactly as planned for any of the adults who work in the building.

What we can almost never plan for is the time, place, and severity of a student misbehaving. Some of the misbehaviors are momentary and ignored by the adults. Others require the adults to redirect the student gently and firmly to the task at hand. Periodically, the misbehavior begins to disrupt lessons or orderly transitions through the hallways and cafeterias and playgrounds. The nearest adult is expected to act. But what action is advisable here and now? And how long will it take, amid all the other students who need that adult's attention and oversight? What about those plans the adult had for this time? Whose job is it to deal with this student now?

Too often, we don't have answers to those questions, despite the fact that these flashpoints of stress and tension happen thousands of times a year. Schools have many routines, customs, and legal requirements, but student misbehavior can slip and slide through all those structures—almost by definition. Significant misbehavior is outside of what the adults have planned for the day.

So, the nearest adults step in to intervene without a plan, knowing that once they begin to engage in an intervention, there is no turning back—the student must be dealt with until they change the misbehavior. To do less would be a serious breach of responsibility. Some adults have developed a reliable set of professional tools that usually meet the moment; others begin to sound like they are at their wits' end (where they likely are), and the situation escalates into a bad one for the students and the adults involved. They raise their voices. They deliver warnings. When nothing else works and time is becoming an issue, the adults have one last tool at the bottom of their kit: they send the student to "the office."

NO ONE KNOWS WHAT HAPPENS AT THE OFFICE. IT'S A BLACK BOX OF POWERFUL INTERVENTIONS.

No one knows what happens at the office. It's a black box of powerful interventions. The "office" may also be an administrator arriving on the scene, summoned with a walkie-talkie. No one knows what this administrator will do, except that they must have a more powerful set of tools and apparently nothing else on their agenda for the hour.

Sometime later in the same class time, or the day, or the next day, the student returns, perhaps with an apology. The incident has taken time away from whatever all the adults might have been doing while dealing with the student. The student has missed instruction time. No more precious time will be devoted to this incident.

I have talked with scores of school administrators and teachers about these moments of stressful decision-making when students misbehave and act out. Teachers relate how anxious they feel when they must call the office. They do not know if administrators will question them for that decision or strongly affirm them. They wonder if they could have de-escalated the situation before it reached the point when they had to bother the administrators. They wonder whether the decision to send the student to the office will be negatively referenced in their evaluation; they *never* expect such a decision will be positively referenced in their evaluation. They often don't know what happens in the office or what further responsibilities for intervention, if any, they now have with this student.

Commonly, many teachers are concerned that the student receives only a gentle reprimand when a more significant intervention was called for—or that the student was rewarded by spending time with a warm and friendly counselor who is not a disciplinarian. They worry that the student told only their side of the story, leaving the administrator with concerns about the teacher. They wonder if the office knows the backstory of trauma and failure in this student's life and that similar misbehavior will likely reemerge from the demands of the curriculum on this student. They wonder if the administrators remember how hard it is to teach. The incident may be settled, but the teacher's concerns about their role in the eyes of the administration remain unresolved.

There is a flip side to those concerns for the teacher. They can also worry that an impatient and overworked administrator will be far too harsh with their student. If the administrator doesn't know the backstory of trauma and failure in this student's life, then the teacher may wish they could direct the situation to the compassionate and wise counselor who best knows how to work with this student—but they have no authority to do so. They want the student back as soon as possible and can imagine the student sitting on a bench in the office, filled with guilt, shame, indignation, and fear, waiting endless minutes until the door to the principal's office swings open and they rise to meet their fate. The incident may be settled when the student returns, but the teacher's concerns about the mental health of the student have not been settled. The teacher may be reluctant to send this student back to the office when the next incident emerges.

The administrators have a different set of concerns. They often wonder why the student was sent to the office for a behavior that could (or should) have been dealt with in the classroom. They wonder if the teacher knows that every time they send a student to the office, they are taking away valuable time from tasks that only the administrator can accomplish to keep the school running smoothly. Each teacher seems to have a different and inconsistent set of tolerances. The administrators don't know how the incident unfolded and what part of the story demands an administrative response. They may choose to contact an adult at home and are frustrated that, often, their first interaction with the home will be a negative one. Or perhaps they have already been involved with a series of unsatisfying communications with adults at home, so even though they feel compelled to make the call, they fear the situation will escalate.

Perhaps implicitly, the administrators think that most teachers want them to instill fear into the heart of the student so the student will stop misbehaving—and the administrators know such tactics can backfire, leading to the student shutting down. The administrator may feel compassion, choosing to give this overwhelmed student time to become calm before offering a little pep talk to do their best for the rest of the day. The incident may be settled when the student returns to class, but the administrator's concerns about the relationship between the student and the teacher, and their limited time and capacity to make positive changes for all involved, have not been settled.

One more group remains unsettled by the entire incident: the rest of the students in the class. They have seen their teacher become annoyed, if not angry—and they have also seen other times when the teacher calmly de-escalated a similar situation. They have seen other teachers respond in many ways to such incidents. They have seen a peer—perhaps a good friend—at their worst, with no chance to be helpful. As the teacher tries to pull the class back to the lesson, the students may be preoccupied by their concerns for their peer. They also may be concerned for their own safety if the student quickly returns as if nothing has happened and with no new controls in place. When the student does return, none of the other students know what was done at the office, how their friend is feeling, or if they can do anything to be helpful now.

THE HACK: ESTABLISH EXPECTATIONS

The first step in establishing a calmer and more predictable system of interventions is to create a list of behaviors that demand an administrative intervention; every adult in the school needs to know the list. The list provides clarity that greatly eliminates uncertainty about whether you are the staff person who must handle this situation or if it belongs to the work of another member of the staff, making all these moments far less stressful. Teachers should know for sure that when they send a student to the office or call for an administrator to come for a student, they will be *absolutely* supported for doing so. The administrators need to know that when a staff member refers a student to them, there is no question that they need to intervene.

Of course, students will misbehave at times in completely unpredictable ways, and the adults who are with the students will need to make spontaneous decisions about what to do and who to call, if anyone. These need to be the exceptions. For instance, when I was an administrator, I came across an extremely frustrated student who expressed his frustration by banging a school camera tripod against a door. When he saw me approach, he stopped the banging. I asked him for the tripod, and he gave it to me, luckily unbroken. The student said, with much anguish, "What's going to happen to me?" I sighed and said, "I don't know. I've never come across a student banging a door with a tripod that did not break. I will get back to you about the consequences."

THE FIRST STEP IN ESTABLISHING A CALMER AND MORE PREDICTABLE SYSTEM OF INTERVENTIONS IS TO CREATE A LIST OF BEHAVIORS THAT DEMAND AN ADMINISTRATIVE INTERVENTION.

Who can predict everything our students will do as they try to manage their frustrations with limited coping strategies? But these situations should be the exception, not a daily test of patience and competence. Most often, we know the most common categories and specific actions that require adult responses and interventions. By operating within a clear set of boundaries, trust between the administrators and staff improves greatly, which means we trust each other to handle those exceptional situations.

Here is a sample list of student behaviors that, in many schools, require an administrative response. The list does not include the illegal activities that administrators are required to report to greater authorities; however, there may be schools in which detailing those behaviors supports a safer and more predictable school community. As I discuss later in this chapter, this list should be specific to the needs of each school.

Sample list of student behaviors that require an administrative response:

- Harming themselves or others
- Fighting or other verbally or physically threatening behavior
- Using racist, sexually explicit, or hurtful language, or repeated teasing
- Swearing at somebody
- Vaping, weapons, drugs, alcohol
- Destroying property
- Unreasonable class disruptions
- Skipping class
- Cheating and plagiarism
- Theft
- Major technology infraction
- Ignoring multiple staff expectations to stop behaviors

The list in each school must include what *absolutely* demands administrative contact for intervention—regardless of the students involved or the staff's comfort level with those students. This step allows the school team to deal directly with a significant incident of student misbehavior—to put all its efforts toward safely and compassionately de-escalating the situation without the distraction of wondering who was responsible. Later on, the school team will have time to understand and learn what preventive measures might reduce the repetition of this misbehavior. In Hack 2, we consider administrative options for responding to these behaviors, for they all dictate a response. For now, the school must establish that, regardless of which students and staff are at the scene, the administrators will be involved.

The last item on the sample list—ignoring multiple staff expectations to stop behaviors—may be essential to any list your school develops. Maintaining a safe and focused learning environment is among the most important responsibilities of the staff, and only the staff member in that moment with those students can assess when the learning environment is at risk. In some situations, the list may identify a specific number of times in every school context that students are given the expectation to choose a different behavior before an administrator is involved. The expectation may be individualized for students who need a break from the class before they have exhausted their ability to conform to expectations. As you will see in the next Hack, the administrator's intervention is not about punishment but about finding the best solutions for the situation.

WHAT YOU CAN DO TOMORROW

FOR ADMINISTRATORS:

- **START THE CONVERSATION.** Via email, a full staff meeting, or a smaller meeting in the school, let everyone know that you are establishing clarity about which student behaviors demand administrative intervention.
- **DEVELOP A FIRST DRAFT.** Send out a first draft of the list and ask for feedback. Encourage grade-level or content-level teams to discuss the list and reply all together. The ultimate goal is to create a system

that has significant buy-in and follow-through by the staff who will be implementing the process day to day.

- **REACH OUT TO STAKEHOLDERS.** In some communities, administrators may want to share the list with the superintendent's office, the school committee, or the parent association. Consider pulling the district principals together to generate a list that is vertically aligned with the developmental needs of students in all the schools and supports the mission of the district. Decide who in the community adds value to your work and bring them into the process. Here is a sample email that you may want to send to introduce your intentions:

  Dear ____________,

  Our school is beginning a process to establish a more comprehensive, predictable, and effective system of responding to student misbehavior. By establishing such a system, incidents of student misbehavior will more likely be handled calmly and compassionately, be less likely to disrupt teaching and learning and be less likely to reoccur.

  The step we are taking now is to establish which behaviors require an administrative intervention. We are sharing a draft list of those behaviors with you and other stakeholders so that the list can most thoroughly reflect the concerns and values of our community and support networks.

  Please take a moment to review the list and reply with questions or suggestions for edits–we will be happy to provide more information. We will also share drafts of the next steps in the process, such as behaviors that require a staff response and ways we will respond to such behaviors.

Thank you very much for taking the time to continue supporting our school.

FOR STAFF:

- **START A CONVERSATION WITH ADMINISTRATORS.** Many school leaders don't realize that you want more clarity about which behaviors require their involvement. Get the conversation rolling and suggest co-creating a list of such behaviors.
- **SHARE A FIRST DRAFT OF YOUR LIST.** Generate a first draft of the list to share with the administration, letting them know that it would create more cooperation and agreement between all involved.
- **REACH OUT TO YOUR PEERS.** In the absence of administrative support for this process, a grade-level or subject-area team can develop a custom list to create a more consistent set of expectations for their students.

A BLUEPRINT FOR FULL IMPLEMENTATION

STEP 1: Build a committee.

The best way to establish clarity and unity is to build a committee responsible for developing first drafts, carrying out test runs, and advocating among their colleagues for the implementation of this new system. This team should represent a wide range of staff members. Too often, however, such committees are filled only with counselors and specialists; these people do essential work with students and staff but are not stationed where most negative or challenging behaviors take place—the classrooms. The committee needs an abundance of teachers who are most responsible for addressing student behaviors hour by hour.

I highly recommend that the committee include a couple of no-nonsense teachers who maintain well-organized classes and may be skeptical of a loss of discipline in any new system. The buy-in and advocacy from these strong, though initially skeptical, teachers will help other teachers be open to what is ultimately developed: an expanded notion of discipline that improves student behavior. Let the school community know who is on the committee.

STEP 2: **Lean into the most compelling data.**

Make clear to the staff the concerns that are driving this initiative. Schools compile formal data about critical incidents, referrals to the office, detentions, and suspensions. They may also gather informal data on the frequency teachers are interrupting student misbehavior, the number of times they required a student to see them during lunch and before or after school because of misbehavior, and how often they contacted an adult at the student's home. A critical goal of the initiative is to reduce the frequency of misbehavior while gaining back instructional time. Collect baseline data and share it with the school community.

STEP 3: **Distribute a timeline.**

It is important to create a timeline of how the new system will unfold (see the following sample). The staff need to know where and when administrators will seek their input. In general, people are more willing to support a new initiative if they know the process is thorough and inclusive—the opportunities for staff input must be clearly embedded in the timeline.

A timeline also assures the staff that they will not be expected to suddenly be proficient in a new system—there will be time to practice and to give the committee feedback. Give staff adequate time and support before the new job expectations take effect. Such forethought reduces anxiety and increases buy-in.

This sample timeline allows for an entire year to develop the complete plan, with full implementation happening in the second year.

SAMPLE TWELVE-MONTH HACKING SCHOOL DISCIPLINE TOGETHER TIMELINE

September–October (Hack 1)

- Develop a Hacking Discipline Committee.
    - Establish schoolwide goals for hacking discipline.
    - Identify data points that will illustrate progress.
    - Draft the list of misbehaviors that require administrative involvement.
    - Begin test runs of Hack 1, collecting and sharing stories and data.
    - Finalize and distribute the Hack 1 protocols to staff.

October–November (Hack 2)

- Draft the list of administrative responses to misbehaviors.
- Begin test runs of Hack 2, collecting and sharing stories and data.

- Finalize and distribute the Hack 2 system to staff.

November–December (Hack 3)

- Develop a first draft of reentry plans for misbehaving students.
- Begin test runs of Hack 3, collecting and sharing stories and data.
- Finalize and distribute the Hack 3 system to staff.

December–January (Hack 4)

- Identify structures and procedures that can reduce student misbehavior.
- Solicit suggestions from the entire staff.
- Collect baseline data on the frequency of incidents.
- Identify quick fixes and longer-term improvements.
- Test quick fixes; collect staff feedback and data, and adjust.
- Develop plans to address the most pressing structural and procedural issues.

January–February (Hack 5)

- Draft the list of misbehaviors that are the staff's responsibility.
- Begin test runs of Hack 5, collecting and sharing stories and data.
- Finalize and distribute the Hack 5 system to staff.

February–March (Hack 6)

- Draft the list of staff responses to misbehaviors.
- Begin test runs of Hack 6, collecting and sharing stories and data.
- Finalize and distribute the Hack 6 system to staff.

March–April (Hack 7)

- Share stories, survey staff, and collect data on Hacks 1–6.
- Analyze feedback to make adjustments.
- Present to full staff about the new discipline model, including training, support, and infrastructure to be in place for the next school year.
- Continue to test run the Hacks and continue to report the results back to staff.

April–May (Hack 8)

- Share lists of classroom-based prevention strategies.
- Use feedback to expand and disseminate strategies.
- Begin test runs of Hack 7, collecting and sharing stories and data.
- Finalize and distribute the Hack 7 list of prevention strategies to staff.

May–June (Hack 9)

- Start test runs of the data collection system, collecting and sharing stories and data.
- Distribute manual for inputting data.

June–August (Hack 10)

- Prepare a full implementation plan to start in the new year.

OVERCOMING PUSHBACK

Hack 1 is the first step in a process of creating a better system of responding to student misbehavior. Many staff members will need to hear multiple times that they have a voice in the planning and that the administration will continue to adjust the system through dialogue. Pushback is better than silence when it is viewed as feedback, providing insights into staff concerns.

If I call an administrator, they'll think I can't manage my class or am not doing my job. In the absence of the list, all teachers are vulnerable to that concern any time they seek administrative support. With a shared list of expectations in place, the teacher will now be clearly doing their job when they call an administrator. The teacher and administrator may need to discuss prevention strategies (see Hack 4, Hack 6, and Hack 8) as part of debriefing the incident, but the call in the moment is the absolute right thing to do.

When I have a good relationship with the student, I don't want an administrator who may not handle the situation as well as I can. Some teachers do have such strong relationships with students that they can effectively de-escalate many incidents. They should be affirmed for their skills. Let them know that even when an administrator has been summoned or the student has been sent to the office, the teacher retains an important role in the process of any incident; the stronger their relationship with the student, the larger the role they will play.

As you will see in Hack 5, staff will also retain full responsibility for most daily behaviors. The behaviors on the administrator's list are larger issues of safety and equity that require additional time to investigate, contact others involved, call the student's home, and track on the school's database.

I want to be trusted to call in an administrator whenever I don't have time to deal with student misbehaviors. Many times, a staff member will happen upon student misbehavior on their way to a meeting or to teach a class, for example. They know the situation needs to be resolved, but they cannot take on that responsibility in the moment. They should be affirmed for their commitment to being focused on their work and for contacting the office so the incident can be settled. The goal of the new system is not to catch staff members making mistakes. Everyone improvises in the moment, but when the new system is functioning, those moments will be a tiny minority of times compared to the calm and predictable implementation of the system. If a staff member consistently does not follow the system, it is treated in the same way as other performance expectations.

Administrators are too busy to address student misbehaviors. The problem is usually the opposite. Administration is already addressing many behaviors they would rather the staff handle. Decreasing those more minor involvements will allow administrators to focus on the more significant misbehaviors that they truly must handle. The effort to carefully develop the list of misbehaviors that belong to the main office will result in the administrators' handling of misbehaviors that are truly in their purview to address—no more and no less than that. In most schools, it will be a significant improvement to the confusion and frustration that previously existed.

THE HACK IN ACTION

At the K–8 Brown School, the administration had a hectic day, with a number of students sitting on the bench in the main office because of misbehavior. When the school day was over and the building was quiet, Assistant Principal Maria knocked on the door of the principal, Anna, and said, "I don't think half the students sent to the office today had to be sent to us. The teachers could have handled a lot of these situations in the classroom."

Anna replied, "Perhaps … but we have no agreement in the school about when students need to be removed from class—other than if there is a fight or if it's necessary to call the police. My guess is the teachers aren't sure when we want to see students to address specific behaviors. That's not their fault; it's the system we all inherited. Are you and I even in agreement about when students should be sent to the office?"

Anna and Maria immediately began to write a list of the student behaviors that would absolutely require an administrative response, either through calling the administration or sending a student to the office. Anna and Maria quickly discovered they viewed what should be on the list differently. They talked through the differences, which reflected their own years as teachers, their tolerance for certain student misbehaviors, and their daily priorities as school leaders. They found their dialogue fascinating.

"This is what we have to do with the staff, too," Anna said. "I learned from this conversation. You and I weren't on the same page, but to send out this list now as a done deal would be a mistake—too much top-down decision-making. This list feels clear to us, but sending it out now wouldn't result in nearly as much buy-in as we need. And the teachers may have reasons to edit the list from their experiences."

Maria agreed. "I think we should pull together a committee to get their opinions and to give us ideas from their teams and departments. I am already imagining who I would want to see sitting around the big conference room table, listening to each other and giving us their recommendations. This could be interesting and good for all of us to find common ground. Can you imagine Mr. L and Ms. V working together?!"

"Mr. L would be really interesting to have on the committee," Anna mused. "He's old school and a department head, but the students really respect him, and so does the staff. And Ms. V may seem like a permissive art teacher, but the kids really respect her, too. Those two may not be as different as they first seem. In fact, they could be the foundation stones of the committee if they don't blow it up."

During the next two weeks, Anna and Maria took a few actions. They emailed everyone the data on how many students had been sent to the office in the past year and categorized the reasons. In the email, they shared that they wanted to be sure everyone in the school knew which behaviors were the responsibility of staff members to handle—and acknowledged that the lack of such clear boundaries contributed to stress in the school community.

They asked for volunteers to be on a committee to make recommendations for what should be on the list of misbehaviors requiring administrative interventions. Included in that email was the preliminary list of behaviors they had developed, with the word "DRAFT—to be reviewed by the committee and the staff" at the top of the list, bigger than all the other fonts. Anna assumed the responsibility of reaching out to Mr. L, and Maria took on the task of reaching out to Ms. V, and both teachers agreed to give the committee a try.

Within a month, they filled a committee with a wide variety of teachers and a strong handful of specialists. They received feedback from many teachers about the draft list of misbehaviors, with more than a few thanking them for addressing this issue. Perhaps coincidentally, starting when they sent out the draft list, they saw a significant drop in the number of students sent to the office. Anna and Maria knew that drop was likely a short-lived response to everyone being more aware of their decisions—far more work would be needed to create sustained changes to the long-standing culture of the school. Finally, they set a date for the first meeting.

Student misbehavior is as much a part of every school day as taking attendance or assigning homework. What's less common is for all adults in the school to know for sure which of those misbehaviors are the domain of administrators and which are the responsibility of the rest of the staff. In the tense moments when a situation with students escalates, without clarity about what staff should do on their own, the safety and security of all involved is at risk.

The hack to this problem starts with conversations among the adults in the school and drafts of lists that begin to define the boundary between administrative and staff responsibilities for discipline. A successful hack clarifies the processes to manage significant misbehaviors and builds stronger bonds among the adults.

For Administrators:

- What are the compelling reasons that necessitate your involvement in student misbehaviors?
- Which staff members can give you quality feedback on a first draft of those misbehaviors?
- Which members of the school community may need direct contact with you to understand your goals for the school as you hack discipline?

For Staff:

- When would you most want an administrator to intervene in student misbehaviors?
- Which student misbehaviors might be hard for you to cede to an administrator, even if your peers found consensus to do so?
- If the administrators asked for volunteers to be on a Hacking Discipline Committee, what factors would you weigh in deciding whether to volunteer?

HACK 2

BE MORE THAN A HAMMER

DEVELOP A TOOLKIT OF ADMINISTRATIVE RESPONSES

If the only tool you have is a hammer, it is tempting to treat everything as if it were a nail.
— ABRAHAM MASLOW, PSYCHOLOGIST

THE PROBLEM: WHAT HAPPENS IN THE OFFICE IS A MYSTERY

SCHOOL ADMINISTRATORS HAVE more hierarchical power than the rest of the staff, but they don't have unlimited power to meet all challenges all the time. They work at the intersection of the infinite needs of their students and the finite resources made available to them—a struggle teachers face as well. One result of the gap between needs and resources in schools is that most students do not reach mastery in their coursework. This means that in the face of their academic struggles and other vulnerabilities, many begin to misbehave. By high school, millions of students drop out of school every year.

Organizations ultimately give us the outcomes they were built for, and unfortunately, our schools are rooted in accepting a huge amount of failure. Many gains have been made since the 1960s when the dropout rate hovered around 25 percent. The dropout rate now is currently just above 5 percent (although with great disparity among historically vulnerable communities, ethnic groups, and disability groupings). Legislation in special education and equal access to the curriculum has supported the success of many marginalized students. But those 5 percent still dropping out represent millions of people at great risk. Every story of a student dropping out is unique to the individual, but collectively, those stories remind us that dropping out is often a process that unfolds over years of alienation and failure—not a single event.

DETENTIONS, SUSPENSIONS, AND EXPULSIONS—THE BIG RESPONSES MOST OFTEN IN THE TOOLKITS OF ADMINISTRATORS—ARE INEFFECTIVE IN CREATING POSITIVE OUTCOMES.

For many students, the punitive response by the school to their misbehaviors becomes accumulating events of alienation, even for those who make it to high school graduation. The era of unrestrained corporal punishment is largely gone (sadly, it is still legal in seventeen states), not only because hitting children is cruel but because such extreme responses have proven to be ineffective in student achievement. Detentions, suspensions, and expulsions—the big responses most often in the toolkits of administrators—are equally ineffective in creating positive outcomes. Instead, they foster further alienation from the daily work and expectations of the school. Studies on the causes of students dropping out—particularly students of color—point to frequent detentions, suspensions, and expulsions as counterproductive to creating a better school climate. Quite simply, our historical practices of punishments that shame and exclude don't work.

All that history and concern weigh on every adult's response when students break the rules—from minor misbehaviors to significant disruptions—and most significantly, they weigh on school administrators when a student is sent to the office. The office remains the place to go for receiving a more significant punishment than the teacher is allowed to inflict. Administrators make crucial decisions in those moments when students come to the office, and cumulatively, those decisions can impact students for a lifetime.

Being the ultimate disciplinarian for the school, having the big hammer in one's hands to impose punishment is rarely the motivation to become a school leader. However, it seems to be how schools have always been organized, so many leaders reluctantly play that role. School leaders also know that teachers will judge them on how strongly they have impacted the student sent to them. Meting out a detention or suspension can send a strong message to the staff that their concerns have been addressed, even when the data of long-term results for many students says otherwise. In the hurly-burly rush of activity that is the norm in schools, the doling out of a detention or suspension is shorthand for "The student has been punished. I supported you."

Part of the dilemma for school administrators who seek other strategies in responding to the misbehaving student is that they are often no more equipped than the classroom teacher to spontaneously craft an alternative to punishment. Their training to be an administrator did not include a more abundant toolkit of responses for student misbehavior than when they were teachers. They are also in the midst of other tasks—just like with the teacher, the student's behavior is an interruption. They may only have a marginal relationship with the student, or worse still, only know the student from their trips to the office. A deeper dive into the background of the student and the current misbehavior is time-consuming. And the administrators certainly will need to share with the teachers their nonpunitive strategies and convince the teachers of their efficacy versus detention and suspensions, but there is no system in place to do all that. Pulling out the hammer of punishment is at least quick and well-established, if nothing else, and if all you have is a hammer, everything begins to look like a nail.

THE HACK: BE MORE THAN A HAMMER

After establishing the school's boundaries for which behaviors must be managed by the teachers in the classroom and which belong to administration, the next step is to provide the administration with a diverse set of responses.

What must be made explicit to the school community is that no student will "get away" with bad behavior. *All misbehaviors are addressed* in ways that meet the students where they are and communicate with them in ways that are most likely to reduce the repetition of those behaviors. When three students fail a test, we examine the causes of their failure, and each will get an individualized response that supports them in doing better. The same is true when students fail to choose good behaviors because of their concerns, needs, and fears. Every student deserves a response that helps them learn to do better.

The responses must fall into the "Three Rs of Discipline": Respectful, Reasonable, and Related.

Respectful: Just because a student has misbehaved, even significantly, does not mean they are now vulnerable to the adult power to shame, ridicule, and intimidate. In the moments when students know they have done poorly and they have been sent to the office for what they are sure will be punishment, our ability as adults to remain steadfast and respectful is one of the biggest lessons they will learn in how to deal with strong emotions. They will also implicitly learn that we want them to remain in our community.

Reasonable: In the office, all the power lies with the adults. We can assign any response we want within legal boundaries. In the absence of a well-prepared set of responses that are supported by the staff, an overly punitive response—such as multiple days of detention—gives the impression of firmness. If we don't know what else to do, we assign more of what we can do, even if we doubt it will work. What unreasonably harsh punishments don't do is provide the student with better tools to handle their issues. The message sent to the student may be to not get caught next time. In contrast, a reasonable punishment is like a good lesson plan: it is within the student's capacity to understand and put it to good use.

Related: When a student kicks over a trash can in frustration, and the trash ends up all over the floor, have them clean up the trash. One mantra from the restorative discipline movement is to not focus as much on the rule that was broken as on the harm that must be repaired. So often, the harm that must be repaired is in the trust that was damaged. Cleaning up the trash allows the student to make right what they harmed and, in that process, to be made whole again. An unrelated response, such as the loss of a field trip or the assigning of detention, does not pull the student back into the good graces of the community, but fixing the harm—cleaning up the trash—allows the student to experience our forgiveness.

EVERY STUDENT DESERVES A RESPONSE THAT HELPS THEM LEARN TO DO BETTER.

The response list for administrators dealing with student misbehaviors needs to be crafted to match the mission, resources, and culture of the school community. The list does need to contain the traditionally most powerful responses, from calling the police to seeking another placement. A safe school environment is ultimately the responsibility of the school leaders, and they must continue to be empowered to take such decisive steps. However, those steps are now just a small fraction of the tools the community asks the leaders to consider.

Sample list of administrative responses to student misbehavior:

- administrative conference
- parent contact
- lunch detention
- in-school suspension
- out-of-school suspension
- referral to counseling
- loss of privileges, with a plan to regain them
- apology: in writing or in person
- peer circle
- restitution to fix damage
- community service
- Chill-Out Plan (see Hack 8)
- mediation
- reflective writing
- research presentation about a related topic to the class or assembly
- read a book to a peer about a related topic
- referral to another program
- police called

In the list, one of the options is peer circles, as described in *Hacking School Discipline*. It's a foundational piece in many schools committed to restorative discipline practice. Peer circles allow an entire class or similar group, such as a team, club, or set of friends, to discuss the impact their peer's action had on them and then be able to tell their peer exactly what those impacts were. This is most often facilitated by a trained staff member. The peers may also be able to share in developing the restorative actions they want their peers to take in order to repair the harm done to them. Peer circles are powerful tools for restoration. Circles are not used only when a student misbehaves but for any activity or situation in which peers sharing with peers supports a higher-functioning program.

Developing such a culture of peer circles as a schoolwide practice is a multiyear process, first involving the training of the adults, who begin to use circles in their staff and department meetings. Circles are introduced to the classroom culture as a common routine; when a crisis of misbehavior occurs, the students will have already had much practice in how to conduct themselves in the rituals of a circle.

The inclusion of peer circles in the list is specifically for those schools that have had the training and have been using circles in their culture. I have worked with many teachers who, on their own, built such a culture in their classrooms, and they should certainly be encouraged to continue their practice. However, if peer circles are not embedded in a school's practices, they should not be considered as a tool for when a student has misbehaved and been sent to the office.

WHAT YOU CAN DO TOMORROW

FOR ADMINISTRATORS:

- **DISCUSS YOUR UNIQUE PERSPECTIVES.** Share what you want to include in the options list for responding to student misbehaviors. The conversation should clarify what you already have as a practice, what you can realistically implement, and what you aspire to be able to implement. The opportunity to utilize more than "the hammer" in responding to student misbehavior may allow all the leaders to prioritize their responses and the distribution of tasks and perhaps to seek resources to do this work in a way that more fully meets the mission of the school.

- **SHARE WITH STAFF.** Disseminate a draft of behaviors that require administrative involvement. In the absence of a standing committee working on hacking discipline, before disseminating the draft, administrators can first seek the input of a few influential staff members–and not necessarily only those who would immediately be supportive of the options on the list. This step better ensures that an important option has not been overlooked and can give the administration insight into framing certain points to best be considered by the staff. The inclusion of those staff members at this time also lets the rest of the staff know the process is truly seeking robust input.
- **START YOUR DATA COLLECTION.** Begin tracking the responses you use when dealing with student misbehavior. In most schools, it is mandatory to track the data on suspensions, referrals, and expulsions. Starting to collect data on all the other interventions will give insight into the current practices of the administrators, allowing them to compare their

choices and track changes in their responses as they continue to fine-tune their efforts.

FOR STAFF:

- **COMMUNICATE YOUR INTEREST IN BEING PART OF THE SOLUTION.** In the absence of a formal system of communication between administration and staff, tell the main office how you want to be involved in the intervention with the misbehaving student. You may want to sit with the administrator as they develop a response. You may want to call the student's home. The school may not always have the time and resources to grant your requests, but you are more likely to achieve the involvement you desire by communicating that clearly.
- **ASK FOR TIME TO DEBRIEF WITH THE ADMINISTRATOR.** When a student is sent to the office for misbehavior, there are often many questions about the event, including the decision-making of all the adults involved, and what can be done to prevent a recurrence with the student. In the absence of answers to those questions, the adults involved may vary greatly in their conclusions, often leading to future miscommunication. Be proactive in seeking out a follow-up conversation with the administrator who worked with the student.

A BLUEPRINT FOR FULL IMPLEMENTATION

STEP 1: Refine drafts of the administrators' options list.

Changing long-standing school practices requires a commitment to transparency in the process.

A January 2003 article in *Harvard Business Review* by W. Chan Kim and Renée Mauborgne, titled "Fair Process: Managing in the Knowledge Economy," states that "employees will commit to a manager's decision—even one they disagree with—if they believe that the process the manager used to make the decision was fair." There has been so much top-down decision-making regarding school reform, curriculum changes, and staffing usage through the years that many staff members have a well-earned resistance to more change—even if they like the vision and the plan. The Hacking Discipline Committee, with its relationships to those doing the work throughout the school, is the best mechanism to thoroughly vet the administrators' options list.

In the absence of a committee, a team of administrators can distribute drafts of their options list. As each successive draft is shared, the administration can provide a summary of the input they received from staff and how that input influenced their decision-making. This step of transparency once again communicates that a fair process is driving the work, predicting a much greater level of buy-in for implementation.

STEP 2: Hear directly from the staff.

Staff need to know that the perspectives of those who do the work have been a significant part of the development of a plan—for some staff, face-to-face conversations carry more weight than providing comments on proposals. Committee members can speak directly to their peers on teams, grade levels, and subject areas to hear concerns and recommendations and bring those back to the committee for a thorough hearing. Gathering peer feedback needn't be formal and data-tracked, requiring undue effort by the committee members. The committee can discuss ways to gather that feedback within the flow of the work week. The committee members will get back to the staff members who raised issues, sharing the outcomes of the committee's discussion.

Administrators can provide multiple means of acquiring feedback: anonymous surveys, meetings with teams and departments, and office hours. In some schools where the trust and lines of communication between administration and staff are not in good shape, the administration will need to be persistent in seeking and reporting feedback, continually making clear the inclusive nature of the process. Trust in all human relationships is built through predictability; make a consistent effort to hear and honor the input of the adults in the school to successfully reform a process or culture.

STEP 3: Standardize the administrators' options list.

Once you have a working draft of the options list, the committee can recommend implementing a test run period (for example, for three months). The committee then gathers data on how the options have been used and reviews outcomes for individual students, for cohorts of students, and for the school as a whole. The committee can then amend the list. After a small number of such test runs, the list becomes standardized as part of the school culture, with perhaps a yearly survey and review to adjust for notable changes.

These steps and the plan for full implementation correspond with the October–November sample schedule listed in Hack 1.

OVERCOMING PUSHBACK

The history of punishment is so deep and long—even if minimally effective—that many staff will worry that a vacuum will be left in its place, leading to chaos. The process of sharing drafts, engaging in conversations, and communicating outcomes will help staff know that a reliable system is in place when punishment is no longer the only response. Here are responses to potential pushback.

We need uniform consequences for rule-breaking so students will think twice about their actions. Many staff believe that uniform consequences reduce student misbehavior. That belief is based on the notion that, in times of crisis, students carefully weigh and measure their actions based on the consequences they face—and that in such a moment, the student has a toolkit of alternative actions to choose from. Far too many students are not so skilled and self-reflective. They receive the predictable consequence without gaining any new tools or insights about themselves for when they next face a similar situation. When the next incidence of misbehavior occurs, the adults are stuck between meting out the same punishment or beginning an escalating series of harsher punishments in hopes of eventually breaking the student's run of misbehavior.

When students break the rules, the school is presented with an opportunity to help them make amends and learn new strategies for coping, and in that process, build a better relationship with the adults who are maintaining school safety. Data on the implementation of such restorative practices in schools shows that they are achieving better outcomes than repeating the same uniform punishments.

It is not fair that different students will receive different consequences for the same behavior. What's not fair is ignoring the needs, skills, and potential for change in every student when giving out a uniform punishment. Schools are learning institutions. We help students improve their behavior when we craft responses that are most likely to teach students new skills and hold them accountable to the community in specific ways. Students can understand that fair treatment is not always the same as equal treatment; adults can understand that as well.

Varying responses to student misbehavior can feed into historic patterns of racism. This is a concern schools must directly confront, as students of color often receive far harsher punishments than their white peers. Students of color may be more often identified as causing trouble and, consequently, more often receive uniform punishments; this process has been labeled the "school-to-prison" pipeline. Unfortunately, uniform punishments are part of that pipeline, and such a process ignores how unexamined prejudice can drive adult observations and decisions. Uniform punishments may feed into the worst aspects of our systems.

The work of the administration and the Hacking Discipline Committee includes tracking the school's records of students being sent to the office so that overall patterns of racial bias can be identified. Similarly, the administration will record the interventions they choose for the students they see for discipline, once again allowing the committee to check on the biases that may influence the work. Treating each misbehaving student respectfully and as an individual, crafting a response that meets the student's capacity to learn and then reporting decisions back to the staff, is a better safeguard against unchecked prejudice than a practice of undifferentiated uniform punishments.

THE HACK IN ACTION

The first meeting of the Hacking Discipline Committee began with a small eruption. Anna, the principal, asked everyone sitting around the big table to share a hope they had for the work ahead. When it was his turn, Mr. L gruffly said, "My hope is that we don't set up a system in which kids are getting away with things more than they are now. Frankly, I think we need a little more discipline around here, a little more effort on everyone's part to hold the kids responsible."

The room fell quiet. Principal Anna and AP Maria had anticipated Mr. L's skepticism that restorative practices would make for a safer school community—that is why they sought his participation. Maria spoke: "Mr. L, thanks for so honestly sharing your perspective. We want that sort of honesty. If our work is going to be successful, we need to hear all the perspectives we can that make up this community."

She continued, "I have Mr. L's permission to share with you all why Anna and I were so excited he joined the committee. Everyone knows that Mr. L runs a tight ship in his room, in his own unique way. His students know what the exact expectations are in his room, and he addresses student misbehavior directly and, most importantly, respectfully and reasonably. Nothing we plan for this committee should undermine his work." Mr. L nodded as Maria spoke.

With introductions and an overview done, the main activity of the first meeting was to review the draft of behaviors that required administrative involvement that Anna and Maria had crafted. They found consensus on many items, especially the most extreme and dangerous behaviors. More questions and concerns were raised about student behaviors that some teachers felt comfortable handling on their own.

Ms. V, the art teacher, spoke up. "For many students, I frankly don't want to send them to the office. I understand the role administration plays in keeping the school safe, but it's a scary thing to be sent to the office to be punished. I'm not interested in kids being punished more often. I don't think punishing kids makes them better learners in the long run." Many heads around the table nodded in agreement.

Principal Anna said, "The vision here is that the main office will be an extension of the work you do in class. Just as you deal with misbehavior based on the context, we can do the same in the main office with your support and trust. I don't think punishing kids makes them better learners either! That's the next item of business for us—to make sure that sending the kids to the office is not about how we powerful administrators mete out harsh punishments. We may need to consider what the word 'punishment' means." She had everyone's attention.

Anna continued, "Let's complete the draft of behaviors that do require the main office to be involved in some fashion—knowing that our involvement is not synonymous with punishment but with choosing the right course of action. Then, we will dive into the options for administrators to use as they respond to misbehaviors. These efforts go hand in hand."

With that framing, the discussion of behaviors that required the main office to be involved became less pressured. The committee came to a loose consensus that sending a student to the office was not seen as a failure of the teacher to handle a situation, and it was not seen as a way to scare a student. Principal Anna said, "I'd like it if students didn't see the main office as a place of punishment but instead as another place to get help to do well. I didn't come into this profession to be a relentless disciplinarian. I want the students to learn that 'being sent to the office' is how we support them, and the stories they hear from their peers who return from the office should help shape that perception."

Ms. K, the school's longtime librarian and one of the most well-liked members of the staff, said, "Getting to talk through this issue with all of you has been quite wonderful, and now I understand what is ahead. We need this sort of conversation all over the school. Everyone needs a chance to think through the reasoning. I'll be happy to type up the new draft of misbehaviors for sending students to the office, and then we can start having those conversations. I'm excited for this."

"Thanks, Ms. K," Maria said. "We'll get feedback from the staff on the behavior list and see what needs changing. We'll implement it for two months, and then we'll review it again before Anna puts her stamp of approval on it."

Anna said, "That brings us to the next draft list Maria and I want to share. It's a menu of options that the main office can choose from when we are seeing a student for discipline purposes. And let's start saying this regularly, around this table and around the school: 'Discipline is not the same as punishment.' You'll see that detentions, suspensions, and even referrals to other programs are on this list because those strong actions must involve administration. But we can take many other actions to support all your efforts when a student comes to the main office. We'll go through this draft with as much honesty and attention as we did the list of misbehaviors. The process will then be the same: we type up the next draft version, talk with the staff, and come back here to revise before we give it a test run."

By sharing their perspectives and options as the school's ultimate disciplinarians, administrators can improve trust and efficiency when everyone is dealing with significant student misbehavior. A Hacking Discipline Committee can provide a forum for administrators to share their stories and concerns and to hear the stories and concerns from the staff. These conversations, along with the data collection from the test runs, allow for fine-tuning the administrative response list. The discussions the committee members have with the rest of the staff continue to break down barriers between the work of the administrators and the work of the staff in maintaining a safe and supportive school environment, even with the inevitable critical events of student misbehavior. No longer is the decision-making of the administration left to speculation when they deal with a misbehaving student. The refrain that staff can "trust administration" will be bolstered by evidence and dialogue.

For Administrators:

- What concerns do you have about changing a school culture of uniform consequences for student misbehaviors?
- Which members of the school community may require face-to-face conversations to understand this new direction in discipline?
- What mechanisms does the school have in place for you to share with staff your decision-making process in choosing responses for student misbehaviors?

For Staff:

- Are you more or less likely to send students to the office for discipline, knowing that the administrators will not be applying uniform consequences?
- When you send misbehaving students to the office, what information do you need in order to trust that the administration is making good choices?
- What advice would you give to the administration to gain staff buy-in for this initiative?

HACK 3

PLAN FOR REENTRY

WALK CALMLY BACK TO THE ROOM

Checklists seem able to defend anyone, even the experienced, against failure in many more tasks than we realized. They provide a kind of cognitive net. They catch mental flaws inherent in all of us—flaws of memory and attention and thoroughness.

— ATUL GAWANDE, SURGEON AND AUTHOR

THE PROBLEM: A LACK OF REENTRY PROTOCOLS CAUSES STRESS

A STUDENT WHO SIGNIFICANTLY misbehaves is sent to the office. What happens when, only a short time later, the student reappears at the door of the classroom? In the absence of rituals of reentry, the student likely returns to their seat looking a bit sheepish or perhaps slightly defiant in an effort to save face. They may give a quick smile to their friends or pull out their workbook, making a show of determination to be on task.

The teacher may not want to give the student too much attention or take time from the lesson. The student's prior behavior has already disrupted the schedule of learning. The teacher wonders whether the student should be left alone to settle in or if the student would feel better if the teacher approached to have a quick word of welcome. There is also the possibility that the student has already gained far too much adult attention for misbehavior, and the better course of action is to move on with no further involvement. Many of the other students may be less focused on the lesson than on how the teacher and the returning student will behave with each other—will there be more drama, more disruption?

THE ABSENCE OF PREDICTABLE RITUALS OF REINTEGRATION LEAVES THE RETURNING STUDENT, THE TEACHER, AND THE REST OF THE CLASS IMPROVISING EACH TIME AN INCIDENT OCCURS.

The absence of predictable rituals of reintegration leaves the returning student, the teacher, and the rest of the class improvising each time an incident occurs. The situation leaves all wondering if their only role is to pretend the original incident never happened.

Reentry is a critical step to reduce anxiety and clear up unresolved issues that may otherwise spark a repeat of the original incident. Each person in the room who was a witness to the original incident has a cognitive and emotional investment in knowing how the situation is resolved and what their role may be in bringing the class back to its usual state.

For the returning student, these are questions that may cross their mind as they return to their classroom. Leaving these unaddressed may only add to the stress, confusion, and potential aggression that can spark future student misbehaviors.

- Is the teacher angry with me?
- How do I let everyone, or anyone, know what happened at the office?
- What do the other students think of me now?

- How will I find out what I missed?
- How do I find out what the class is working on now?
- Can I ask a friend what happened when I was sent out?
- Should I sit at my desk and wait for the teacher to tell me what to do?
- How do I gain forgiveness?

For the teacher, these are questions that undoubtedly occur when a student arrives back to class after a severe disruption.

- Is this student really ready to be back in class?
- What instructions or consequences has this student received?
- What do I do if the student begins to misbehave again?
- Is there a role for me in the plan?
- What do the other students need to know?
- Can I impose my own consequences in addition to what the office put in place?

For the other students in the room, particularly those who may be friendly with the student who was sent to the office, they may be wondering some of the following questions.

- Can I ask my friend if they are okay?
- Can I tell them what happened after they left the room?
- Can I do something to help next time a similar situation occurs?
- How will they catch up on the work they missed?

THE HACK: PLAN FOR REENTRY

In his book *The Checklist Manifesto*, author Atul Gawande observes that in times of stress and complexity, we are at risk of thinking and acting impulsively. A reliable list of steps to use in such situations allows us to make better decisions.

The next step in hacking school discipline is to have an established set of procedures—a checklist, perhaps—for reference through each stage of a student's return to the classroom. Given the endless tasks and unpredictable situations that occur in every school every day, and the time pressure everyone feels to finish those tasks, a reliable system that scaffolds a student's successful reentry to class is highly recommended.

A reliable system of reentry will take into account all the questions listed earlier. The system will include steps that are uniformly followed, regardless of the adults and students involved. Other steps will provide differentiation for the child's developmental capacity; for the history of the relationships between the student, peers, and staff members involved; and for the current activity happening in class when the student returns.

The role of the main office staff is to make sure the student is truly ready to return to class and dive back into the class activity—and not to rush this step of readiness. Administrators often feel an imperative to return a student to class as soon as possible so they don't miss any more of the curriculum. That imperative must be balanced by an equal commitment to assure the sanctity of the learning environment for all. If a quick return once more destabilizes the class, the returning student, their peers, and the teacher will not experience trust in the process, and that imperils all.

The reentry role of the teacher is to assure the student that any plan crafted in the main office will be followed and that the student is truly welcomed back. The rest of the class will want to know if they have a role in their peer's return. They have seen a peer at their worst; knowing their role in the reentry process can teach them compassion and responsibility as community members. For schools that have developed a culture of restorative circles, the class will often circle up as soon as the student leaves the room, and the main office will need to know the outcome of that circle.

WHAT YOU CAN DO TOMORROW

FOR ADMINISTRATORS:

- **DISTRIBUTE A CHECKLIST TO TEACHERS OF WHAT HAPPENS BEFORE STUDENTS RETURN.** Here is an annotated checklist for the main office staff to prepare the student to return to class.
    - The student is given a safe and calming place to wait in the office. Ideally, this is not on a bench in sight of everyone who walks by, which can be unnecessarily shaming or agitating. This is also a time when a school support staff member can be utilized to listen to the student's concerns and help the student de-escalate. The administration can work with the support staff member to be part of this conversation.
    - The administration chooses its response from the list developed in Hack 2.
    - The administration works with the student to understand the reparative work the student will do and the plan to return to class.

- The student is given time to work on any portion of the plan that needs to be done before returning to class. For instance, the student may need to craft an apology, talk to a family member, or begin community service as a form of giving back and earning forgiveness.
- The student is told of the steps to physically reenter the class, and they can, in their own words, repeat the steps back.
- The student is walked back to class with an adult, who continues to support the student in remembering their role in reentering the classroom. If the adult senses that the student is not ready to reenter class–for instance, the student is beginning to argue about their role in returning or speaks belligerently regarding the teacher or peers–the adult does not allow the student back into the room. The adult must make the determination that the learning environment inside the room will not be at risk. If a concern arises, the adult can find a safe place to talk with the student. The student may need more time to de-escalate. The extra time that the staff puts into working with this student will be better spent than risking a recurrence of disruptive behavior.

FOR STAFF:

- **DEVELOP A REENTRY PLAN FOR YOUR CLASS OR OFFICE.** In the absence of a schoolwide list of reentry options, identify the practices that will best work for your setting. This can include peers who will check in with the returning student, or a quiet place for the returning student to sit until there is an opportunity to reintegrate them into the lesson. A quiet place can even be the student's regular seat, where they know they can wait until they are given instructions on how to get back on task. Letting them know that they will be given that support can ease their concerns about what to do while they wait. The sooner they can be given their instructions, the more at ease they and their peers will be, and the focus on the lesson will be improved for all.
- **COMMUNICATE WITH THE MAIN OFFICE.** There may be times when you and the returning student need a couple of minutes to check in before they come back into the room. Let the main office know when such a situation occurs and ask if the person escorting the student back to the room can cover the class for a few minutes so you can have that check-in.

A BLUEPRINT FOR FULL IMPLEMENTATION

STEP 1: Provide options for students to successfully rejoin classes.

During the time the student is in the office developing a plan to return, their peers are often worried for them, as anyone would be if a friend were in distress. Our work in schools includes teaching students how to be responsible members of a community and how to care for their friends—simply telling the class to ignore what happened and return to their textbooks undermines the essential work we do to develop the whole student. The teacher can tell the class that the student is in a safe place in the office to de-escalate and will come back as soon as possible with a reparative plan. If the student has been sent home or suspended, the teacher can let the class know, without breaking confidentiality or causing shame, and again remind the class that as soon as possible, the student will return with a reparative plan. The student's peers need updates.

THE PROCESS TO REPAIR THE HARM IS NOT PUNITIVE BUT RESPECTFUL, REASONABLE, AND RELATED.

Here are options for reentry when the student is at the door of the classroom. No option is better than the others; each needs to be chosen for the resources available at the time and the needs of all involved:

- The student remains in the office until the teacher can have time for a conversation with the student. The conversation can include a counselor or administrator, but the focus of this time is on the teacher and student sharing and planning.
- The adult who has walked the student back covers the class for a few minutes while the student and the teacher talk in the hallway. During this time, the student and teacher discuss the plan for repairing the harm done. The

teacher expresses appreciation for the effort the student has made to de-escalate and to commit to the plan. The teacher may also suggest additional scaffolding to support the student in successfully navigating the difficulties they faced prior to the disruption. The student and the teacher can then come into the room together, a symbolic step for the rest of the class that the problems have been addressed and they can all relax. The teacher and the student can say to the class, "We're good."

- The adult who has walked the student back to class accompanies the student to their seat and stays with the student until the teacher is free to talk with the student.
- The teacher has designated a student in the class who will sit with the returning student to orient them to the work being done until the teacher is free to talk to the student. The designated student should be one who works well with the returning peer. If there is no such student, use one of the prior strategies. What is most critical is that the returning student is not left on their own to figure out what to do next.

Part of the plan developed in the office includes what the returning student will say to their peers who were impacted by the disruption and what the returning student will do to repair the harm done to their peers. This is not a shaming step, since the process to repair the harm is not punitive but respectful, reasonable, and related. The classroom teacher will let the returning student know when they can talk to their peers about the plan.

The options for reentry can be crafted and shared solely by the administration but are best developed by the Hacking Discipline Committee. As I noted in the previous Hacks, the committee is uniquely positioned to share the drafts of new procedures with their peers and, in that process, hear resistance that they may need to overcome as they learn the scaffolding that staff members need to successfully do this unique work.

STEP 2: Offer support to staff for their role in reentry.

A successful reentry to class for a disruptive student must include the participation of the classroom teacher. Quite simply, the work done in the main office cannot repair the teacher-student relationship; when the student's behavior is significant enough to require administrative support, the teacher inevitably has feelings and concerns that must be addressed with the student, too. Students may also reasonably fear that the teacher is unforgivingly angry with them. Upon reentry into class, the other students may also need reassurance that their peer and teacher are okay together. At staff meetings, have staff share their perspectives. Role-play various scenarios. Offer times to meet one-on-one with staff to talk through their concerns and make plans for their situations.

STEP 3: Pilot the process.

As in most steps of hacking school discipline, the committee members are the first staff to pilot a new process. They experience what is working and what needs to be adjusted, bringing their feedback to the committee. They invite other staff members to observe the test runs or to join in. Their commitment to be the first to try procedures and then to signal that the new procedures successfully work in their school is the antithesis of top-down initiatives that have resulted in staff skepticism and resistance—despite the rosy visions that come with those initiatives. Teachers need to hear that their respected peers have vetted the change.

These steps and the plan for full implementation correspond with the November–December sample schedule in Hack 1.

OVERCOMING PUSHBACK

When a student needs to be sent to the office, inevitably, many emotions are stirred up. Oftentimes, those emotions can reduce everyone's capacity to be compassionate and patient through the process of returning a student to class. Building predictable routines and structures into the plans to return students to class can reduce additional stress on top of what has already been experienced. With practice, those routines and structures will reduce pushback.

I don't agree with the plan developed in the office. A perfect plan rarely exists. The feedback of the teacher is critical for the system to develop its integrity and success. Administration needs time to learn how to make the best choices for each student and each situation. The Hacking Discipline Committee can also be the place for reviewing the feedback of teachers and the choices of the administration.

Who has time for this? Every step in the hacking discipline process is designed to reduce the likelihood of the disruptive behavior recurring, which would take up far more staff time than a thoughtful reentry into class. Whether the teacher spends fifteen minutes talking with the student or can only make sure they give the student support to successfully rejoin the lesson, the time spent on prevention is in the teacher's best interests—as well as the best interests of the returning student and all the student's peers.

I don't want to give misbehaving students more attention. One of the most important life lessons the rest of the class learns when a peer has misbehaved is rooted in how we treat the student; they watch the adults to see what compassion, forgiveness, and restorative responsibility look like. The step of reentry is an important moment when all eyes are on the adults to do the right thing, even if only to respectfully help the student return to the work at hand (significant class time does not have to be spent on reentry). Rather than seeing this step as giving more attention to one student, see it as giving attention to the rest of the class as they learn to be responsible members of their communities.

THE HACK IN ACTION

In the first three months since the Hacking Discipline Committee met, they have developed, with robust input from the staff, three working drafts: 1) behaviors that require administrative involvement, 2) a menu of options the administration can choose from to restore a disruptive student to good standing in the community, and 3) a variety of reentry plans for students.

"It's time this committee set up some test runs on our new reentry options," Anna said as she called the next meeting to order, "and so we need volunteers sitting around this table to be part of piloting our work. Maria and I will be handling the students sent to the office. Who wants to partner with us?"

Many hands were raised, including Mr. L's.

"Mr. L, really?" said Ms. K, the well-liked librarian, with a chuckle. "When was the last time you sent a student to the office that you couldn't handle?"

"I don't remember," he replied. "But I want to show support for the work we are doing. I was skeptical. I may still be. Truthfully, a reason I accepted the request that I volunteer for this committee"—he wryly smiled in Anna's direction—"was to make sure we weren't going to be letting kids get away with bad behavior. Now I know that's not the case. I may not need to use this system, but it's going to help a lot of teachers make sure their classes aren't some sort of free-for-all."

Before any of the other committee members responded to Mr. L's statement, Anna jumped in. "Okay, I am seeing all those hands up. That's good. Let's start tomorrow. Ms. K, will you please send a memo to the staff, from the committee, with the names of all the people with raised hands who will be piloting this stage of our work starting tomorrow? Perhaps you can put Mr. L's name first on the list."

"I'll put his name in bold," Ms. K added.

The first call to the office the next day came from Ms. V, the art teacher. Two boys had threatened to fight each other after school; verbal threats and intimidation were on the list of behaviors that demanded immediate administration intervention. Within moments, Assistant Principal Maria was at the door, escorting the two boys to the office.

A half-hour later, Ms. V got the message from Maria that the boys were ready to return to class. Ms. V replied that she was ready and asked that Maria cover the class for three minutes while she checked in with the boys in the hallway. She had also assigned a student to sit with each of the boys when they returned and catch them up on the work being done.

Later that day, she logged on to the hacking discipline tracking form to input her feedback, knowing all the committee members were expected to be reading the feedback forms during this period of test runs. She wrote:

> *The reentry went well overall. The boys had calmed down. They were ready with a short script to let the rest of the class know that they had worked out their conflict and were not going to fight—but also that they did not want to share what they talked about in the office; that was between the two of them. Hearing them share that with the class was the best part of the reentry.*
>
> *One thing I wish had been different was knowing if I had any role to play in the situation. I assumed not, but that wasn't made clear to me. Maybe that could be added to the reentry form, especially if something happened during class that I missed that could have prevented their conflict from escalating. Maybe we need a checkbox to let the main office know when we want a*

follow-up conversation to clarify all that. If communication between administration and staff is a big part of our work, letting teachers know if they have follow-up tasks is super important to build in.

And thanks again to Maria—I never could have handled this situation on my own so well."

The culture of repairing harm versus merely serving a punishment for a broken rule requires time for the student to acknowledge the harm done and to understand how that harm can be repaired. The lesson for the student to learn is not about the consequences of being found guilty but about the place the student holds in the school community and how that place can be restored or improved. Securing this lesson of belonging through a thoughtful reentry into the learning community makes a repeat of similar misbehavior less likely.

For Administrators:

- What shifts in resources may be necessary to consistently provide a well-planned transition of the student back into the school or classroom?
- If all administrators are occupied at the time disciplinary intervention is needed, who will begin the reentry process with the student?
- What professional development training may best help your staff manage their roles in the reentry process?
- How will you obtain feedback from staff to further hone the reentry process?

For Staff:

- When a student returns to class, what do you most want to know about what happened in the office?
- How and when can you share with your class the school's goals for when a peer returns to the class?
- When a student has been sent to the office for misbehaving in your presence, what do you need to do to prepare yourself for the role you will play in their return?

HACK 4

THINK STRUCTURES BEFORE SKILLS

ADDRESS SYSTEMIC PROBLEMS FIRST

Business and human endeavors are systems ... we tend to focus on snapshots of isolated parts of the system. And wonder why our deepest problems never get solved.

— PETER SENGE, SYSTEMS SCIENTIST AND AUTHOR

THE PROBLEM: SPECIFIC TIMES AND PLACES CONSISTENTLY ENGENDER MISBEHAVIOR

SOME CALL IT the original sin of schools: expecting every child born within a twelve-month span to be equally ready to learn the same curriculum on the same day, year after year after year. This is a truly absurd proposition. Combine that absurdity with inequities in opportunities, essential resources, and services from neighborhood to neighborhood, and we get the outcomes we should expect: a huge number of students who struggle to succeed daily. Some of those students freeze, some flee, and some misbehave.

The systemic and developmental advantages of some students over others manifest in more domains than academics. A student who has physically developed ahead of their peers can dominate others on the athletic field through high school; conversely, physically smaller students who might demonstrate a gift for dance may never get the chance to fully explore their talent in school. Students who can discern the emotional state of adults early on, compared to their classmates, are more likely to avoid the displeasure of their teachers and administrators—a huge advantage when seeking help or knowing when to be silent (i.e., not misbehaving).

HACKING DISCIPLINE HAS A PROACTIVE ELEMENT: IT LEADS EDUCATORS TO EXAMINE ALL THE STRUCTURES AND PROCEDURES IN THE SCHOOL THAT INHIBIT THE SUCCESS OF THEIR STUDENTS.

We often see the misbehaviors that result from varied child development in the transition from elementary school to middle/junior high school. The last teachers of an elementary school class know that many of their students are not ready for all the transitions they will face in the coming year, moving from room to room and dealing with the variety of messages, styles, and assignments from teams of teachers. We often see the same difficulties in new high school students, whose underdeveloped executive functioning skills—perhaps more essential for success than cognitive abilities—leave them a step behind their peers in many responsibilities and expectations. Years earlier, kindergarten teachers had feared for the challenges too many of their students would encounter in first grade. The uniform requirement of transitioning within and between schools puts many students at risk of misbehaving.

All those structures, procedures, schedules, and curricula in schools exacerbate the struggles students encounter in their lives outside of education. Collectively, those forces are too much for the coping mechanisms of many young people. In such a cauldron of mismatched expectations and development, we should not be surprised that some students are primed to misbehave. Sadly, the students are the ones who then assume their failures are a result of their being "bad." They are far too young to analyze the entire situation and conclude that their failure may be built into the design of the organization. When an adult's response to their latest misbehavior is "Not again!" no one assumes the adult is referring to the structural dysfunctions of the school.

I must restate an important point here: hacking discipline never ignores student misbehavior, regardless of their developmental and community advantages or disadvantages. Students must learn to manage in their world. Adults must commit to providing coping tools—not punishment. But hacking discipline has a proactive element: it leads educators to examine all the structures and procedures in the school that inhibit the success of their students. The curricula and final exams may be imposed by higher powers, as are the lengths of the school day and year and the rigid grouping of students by age, regardless of their readiness for the task. Given those immovable components, a committed staff can still do much to modify the environment for the greater good, reducing student misbehavior. It's time to hack those problematic structures and procedures.

THE HACK: THINK STRUCTURES BEFORE SKILLS

Leaders of organizations should not spend their money on orienting the staff to work in the idiosyncratic dysfunctions of their systems—they should first develop functional systems and then provide training for everyone to work within those systems. The time and money spent on preventing confusion, errors, and exasperation through streamlining and updating systems will save a tremendous amount of time in dealing with the fallout of inefficiencies.

In my role as a consultant to many school initiatives—from integrating social emotional learning in lesson plans to supporting team teaching to hacking discipline systems—school administrators ask me about the professional development services I can bring to their staff. After we have that conversation, I often ask, "What can you do in your role to make it more likely that the staff will be able to implement and sustain the changes you want to see resulting from my work with them?" That question often leads to a rich and unexplored area of possibilities.

Although school administrators are not omnipotent—everyone is a middle manager of some sort—the administrators have their hands on the movable parts of the system more than any of the other staff—and the perspective to see how all those parts are operating. Before administrators flex their muscles by holding staff and students accountable, they should do all they can to support staff and students to be accountable. They can ask each other, "What can we do first?"

Classroom teachers can do the same within their domains. If students are not implementing routines effectively, even if they've had a lot of practice, it is likely there is a mismatch between the developmental readiness of this cohort of students and the efficient routines that have been in place in prior years. As one of my mentors said to me, "Jeffrey, the students are just being the students. What will the adults do?" Unfortunately, what adults have too often done in reaction to students' behavioral failures is demand and punish. Hacking discipline asks us to do otherwise: first, set up systems so students are most likely to succeed. Teachers who create behavioral routines and systems are less likely to become frustrated and will have more time to teach and enjoy the students.

Many structural problems in the school can be altered without a lot of upheaval. As a principal, when I implemented a quick fix that had a disproportionately positive outcome to the effort I had put into the fix, I often heard from staff, "About time you did that."

When I was a teacher, my students gave me similar feedback when I made a long overdue adjustment to our routines.

In any role in the school, you have a degree of autonomy to adjust routines and structures. Ask yourself and your peers: What changes are within our authority to implement that will minimize persistent misbehaviors?

WHAT YOU CAN DO TOMORROW

FOR ADMINISTRATORS:

- **DETERMINE WHERE AND WHEN MISBEHAVIORS PERSIST.** Take five minutes on your own or with peers and brainstorm the answer to this question: Where and when are students most often misbehaving? To gain the answers to that question, administrators need to take a long and close look at the schoolwide routines and expectations for students entering and leaving the building, in the lunchroom and at recess, for staffing in the hallways–literally any facet of the day that presents persistent problems. It is unlikely you will eliminate misbehaviors, but so often, you can immediately implement steps that will be widely appreciated.
- **IDENTIFY QUICK FIXES.** You need to be a little more judicious than other staff in applying a quick fix; even a small and beneficial change can have unpredictable side effects in a building as large and crowded as a school. You don't have to please everyone, but you should take at least a day to make sure you will not be disrupting a lot of staff. As a principal, even when I knew I was the only one

who had the authority to implement a quick fix and was excited to get the change in place, I made sure to ask a few people if they could imagine the downsides to my ideas. A mentor of mine wisely urged me to wait twenty-four hours before I acted. If the school had been managing, albeit poorly, with the problem for a long time, it made sense to wait a day to act, and it turned out to be wise advice.

Here's one of my favorite stories of a principal noticing a situation that was engendering misbehaviors and applying a quick fix that only the principal could initiate.

The school had a sign-in system for students who were late. The system was extremely cumbersome: students had to wait in line to be signed in and then get a late pass—and any time students are waiting in line, the situation is ripe for misbehavior. The students were also missing even more class time as they waited. The principal asked the director of IT to develop an application to reduce wait times, and a few days later, they inaugurated the new sign-in system: the students tell the office staff their name; the computer application automatically inputs into the database their name, the date, and time of arrival; the printer instantly provides a hall pass with all the information. What once took about a minute per student now took less than ten seconds. On days with many late-arriving students, anyone available in the office—including the administrators—can open the application and help move students quickly through the process.

FOR STAFF:

- **DETERMINE WHERE AND WHEN MISBEHAVIORS PERSIST.** Here are a handful of persistent stressors for students that often lead to misbehaviors. On your own or with peers, identify the ones most in need of adjusting for your current students, or add ones that consistently trigger misbehaviors:
    - routines for when students walk into the room
    - routines for leaving the room
    - protocols for students to gain the floor to speak
    - signals for students to be quiet when you need their full attention
    - signals to ask for help when struggling
    - activities for students who finish work ahead of their peers
    - processes for students who have missed time in class to easily find assignments, handouts, and advice for completing tasks
- **IDENTIFY QUICK FIXES.** You can devise quick fixes for all the structural stressors you identify. While fixing one of them will not completely eliminate misbehaviors, addressing any of these stressors can support your most at-risk students in successfully managing expectations. When you and your peers identify students' persistent stressors, it can be the springboard to sharing the many fixes people

implemented throughout their careers. Much wisdom can be gained through faculty members' experiences. A quick search online can also garner a multitude of fixes. In most cases, the fixes are completely within your domain to apply.

Here is one of my favorite fixes from a middle school teacher:

> The teacher's students had too often been arriving late to their subsequent classes. The teacher recognized that several of her students did not have the time management skills to know how long it would take during passing time to get a drink of water at the fountain, ask another teacher a question, and avoid being late for their next class, which might be at the other end of the building. The teacher instituted a short activity at the end of class: in pairs, the students shared their plans to arrive promptly to the next class, giving each other advice on how to get everything they wanted done and still be on time. The students quickly began looking forward to this activity, and many accepted being on time as a worthy challenge versus a daily stressor. The sharing of plans and often jovial reviews of their successes and failures improved their time management skills, especially for the most at-risk students. As a result, they were less often late to their next class.

A BLUEPRINT FOR FULL IMPLEMENTATION

STEP 1: Support staff in sharing strategies.

In faculty meetings, grade-level meetings, and department meetings, set aside time for staff to brainstorm and share their fixes for the persistent situations in which students misbehave. An online database can catalog those fixes. In some schools with limited meeting times, the database will be the primary place to share staff ideas and stories. The database can be organized into categories, such as transitions, free time, and recess, to support brainstorming and to find the most relevant fixes happening in the school.

STEP 2: Identify the most pressing systemic stressors.

Administrators can use the staff responses to consider more systemic changes rather than considering each situation a result of student or staff failure. The conversations and database can also spark conversations about resources that the administration can provide to implement certain fixes. Administration can propose, through meetings or surveys, the schoolwide fixes within their authority to implement, gaining feedback on details and promoting staff buy-in; transparency in such efforts is almost always a positive enzyme for change.

Through these efforts, I have seen a school fully commit to a single process for gaining an entire class's attention. The process was first implemented by one teacher; her class responded so well that other teachers in her grade adopted the process. The following year, the process followed the students to the next grade—the receiving teachers were appreciative that their students were already accustomed to following a process to be quiet. The following year, the administration leveraged the stories and support of the teachers to propose that the entire school adopt the process. The students now assume that the ways their teachers gain the full class's attention are a natural part of being in school.

STEP 3: Pilot fixes and share stories.

The Hacking Discipline Committee is an excellent place to identify chronic situations of misbehavior through the examination of the collected data. The committee members can pilot fixes, observe the fixes of their peers, adapt them to their own settings, and help build a strong consensus for schoolwide changes.

STEP 4: Seek additional perspectives.

When I was a principal, I had the occasion to walk with an occupational therapist to an IEP (Individualized Education Program) meeting we were both attending. I asked her more about her work, having known embarrassingly little about the field of occupational therapy in schools. In the three-minute walk through the building, she identified sounds, smells, textures, and lighting fixes to support students with sensory difficulties—of which there are many in our schools. The accumulation of irritating sensory input in a school building can decrease almost any student's tolerance of the expectations they must comply with through the long school day, making them more susceptible to misbehaving. The fixes collectively made a more calming environment for every student and adult. Sometimes, the prevention part of hacking discipline is as subtle as the dimming of lights.

These steps and the plan for full implementation correspond with the December–January sample schedule in Hack 1.

OVERCOMING PUSHBACK

I don't know any teachers who would rather spend their time disciplining students for misbehavior than teaching. Reducing the environmental elements that unnecessarily trigger student misbehavior is in everyone's best interest. Conversely, putting students in situations every day that challenge them to use their most tentatively held coping skills is neither compassionate nor productive; it is a setup for adults to be disciplinarians as we deal with students who are not fully capable of managing the system's dysfunctions. As noted at the start of this Hack, staff and students can work within a functioning system that not only alleviates the need for extreme and disruptive disciplinary practices, but it also allows students to feel supported in learning to cope with the consequences of misbehavior in a way that feels forgiving and productive.

The outside world won't accommodate all the needs of students. They must get used to struggling. Many struggles in schools are unnecessary, if not detrimental, to healthy development and learning. For instance, we now provide handicapped-accessible bathrooms versus forcing people with limited mobility to somehow navigate into and out of narrow stalls to simply relieve themselves. We should be discussing which struggles and challenges in our schools engender student strengths and which are merely vestiges of indifference, under-funding, and ignorance. Let's identify which struggles are worth institutionalizing in our practices.

No student should have to "get used to struggling" as a given part of schooling without the adults examining the efficacy of students managing those struggles. Anything that inhibits learning does not belong in the work of schools. We should adjust the most troublesome elements of the school day so students are more ready to do what we want them to do most: engage as fully as they can in the hard and worthwhile task of learning. Successfully mastering the curriculum is a most powerful prerequisite for navigating the inequities and dysfunctions of the outside world. (For practical ideas about engaging students in their learning, read *Even More Hacking Engagement: 50 New Ways to Make Learning Fun for All Students* by James Alan Sturtevant.)

I can't change anything in my classroom or school. Although the words may sound defiant, an educator might say this in full honesty: they don't know what to do. Ask them to share with a peer their list of problematic times and places in order to brainstorm possible solutions. This strategy is also applicable when the speaker is truly resistant to the process. Their resistance may be triggered by long-term frustrations that have nothing to do with the goals of this Hack. Give them a way into the process that does not directly confront concerns about their resistance. They may take longer to apply solutions in order to save face, but they will be working on the issue. Give them the time, ask them when you can circle back to see their improvement, and ask if you can offer any support until then.

I'm not sure most students need these changes. The learned wisdom in schools is that what is necessary for some students is probably good for all. For example, a short break to get up from a desk chair to stretch, a common tactic for students with attention deficits, will help most everyone improve their energy and focus. A door that can open easily for a student in a wheelchair will also open easily for a fully ambulatory student or a teacher carrying books and supplies. Many students manage to cope with the daily dysfunctions in school structures and routines but at a cost to their energy and frustration tolerance. Attending to these dysfunctions will have a positive impact on the productivity of all.

THE HACK IN ACTION

AP Maria walked into Principal Anna's office, her laptop open in her hands, saying, "Have you looked at the statistics from this week's discipline reports? We have got to do something about the cafeteria!"

Anna nodded. "I looked at the statistics this morning. The numbers are probably the same if we had been keeping this data all along."

Maria, clearly upset, said, "Well, there's a bunch of things we can do immediately. We can …"

Anna interrupted her. "You and I are not going to do anything immediately. I mean, not now, not today. The Hacking Discipline Committee meets tomorrow. Let's bring our ideas to them—and let's hear from them before we do anything. Can you wait?"

Maria sighed. "Yeah, because I only have to wait one day until the committee meets."

The next day, after the committee settled in, Maria launched into a review of the discipline reports emerging from the cafeteria. "This is not good!" she said in conclusion.

The room was silent for a moment before Anna spoke: "I know one intervention we all would like to see is to get more staff in there every day. But I looked at what we can do, and there's not much in terms of staffing. Not this year. This committee has taken on looking at structures and processes as much as staffing. Anyway, I am not sure we would want to throw anyone into that chaos in the cafeteria without a better plan."

Mr. P, one of the school's physical education staff, raised his hand. He was the newest staff member on the committee, still in his first year on the faculty, and just out of graduate school. This was the first time he volunteered to speak up.

"I don't mean to sound rude or like I know more than everyone here—I've learned so much already being on this committee—but didn't everyone know the cafeteria was a problem? I didn't want to say anything, figuring someone would mention it. There are lots of things we could do differently … right?"

"Mr. P," Anna said, "I think we did all know, at least implicitly, and I think we've assumed that the environment in the cafeteria will continue to be the same. Or maybe we were all hoping—even me—that somehow, we'd get more staff to cover the cafeteria, thinking that was the only solution. This committee exists to challenge us to do better. Thank you so much for speaking up. We can do lots of things differently—not just one thing."

"So, here's a proposition," Maria jumped in. "Between now and the next meeting, we will talk to everyone we can about how to do lunch better. We bring all the ideas to the next meeting, kick them around, and then Anna and I will put together a proposal. I am betting the staff will be excited we are doing this—or maybe as Mr. P suggested, they'll wonder what took us so long. Let's get on this."

WE MAY COMPLAIN ABOUT THE SYSTEM AND BE AGGRAVATED BY THE STUDENTS WHO MISBEHAVE, AS IF THERE WERE NO CONNECTION BETWEEN THOSE TWO REALITIES.

When the committee next convened to discuss the plan for the cafeteria, Ms. K, the librarian, said, "Just like we predicted, everyone I spoke with about making changes at lunch said, in their own fashion, 'About time!'" Many committee members around the table signaled that they had heard the same.

"Okay, what have we got?" Maria asked.

AP Maria's notes from the meeting included the following:

- Mr. L revealed that he doesn't teach bell-to-bell; he uses the last two minutes for the students to clean up the room. Each week, a different student is assigned to tell him that the room is clean so the students can be dismissed. If the room is ready, he dismisses them. If not, they must figure out what isn't ready. He said that two other teachers in his department told him they have similar rituals. We can do the same with the tables at lunch—one student raises their hand to signal the table is ready to go to recess; the staff person in that area can give them a quick "yes" or "no." We can stop nagging kids about clean-up and make them interdependent.

- Ms. V said she worked in a school in which the students did not go to the food line until their table was called, keeping the time waiting in line short. She reported that Ms. B worked in a school that did a similar system. The kids at the table were provided with games and contests. Mr. D said in his former school, an interesting video played while kids waited at their tables. He said some people with whom he shared this activity didn't like the idea of more screen time, but the idea of keeping the kids busy while they waited made sense to all. Maybe we can have a video day, an "I spy with my little eye" day, a trivia contest day—keep it interesting.
- Mr. P said the gym now has different colored lines. The students are divided into different colored teams, one for each line, and that's where they know to go to start class. He said other PE teachers are piloting this with him. We could divide the cafeteria into color zones and call zones to the line versus table by table. We might do some contests with rewards for the zones and get them to compete to behave well. Okay by me if they all win that contest.
- Ms. R heard from her team of counselors and therapists that many students ask to have lunchtime appointments because they hate the crowd and noise in the cafeteria. She said a peer of hers in another district told her that they have a separate area for kids who want a quiet lunch so they can sit and read or do artwork and just be away from it all. Ms. R's team thinks we should consider this. If we did that, the numbers in the cafeteria would be easier to handle; the quiet lunch area can have a higher student-to-staff ratio—in a way, giving us an extra staff member in the cafeteria.

The next week, Principal Anna sent a draft proposal of changes in the cafeteria to the committee. After some edits, she sent the proposal to the entire staff, including the data the committee would be tracking to see if the changes were working. The administration then planned a two-month pilot run to test the impact of the changes, with a promise to report back to the school community.

Working in a school for more than a few years can inure any administrator or staff person to the possibilities for structural changes. We get accustomed to dysfunction. We may complain about the system and be aggravated by the students who misbehave, as if there were no connection between those two realities. The time spent hacking those structures can have a profound impact on the daily experiences of staff and students.

For Administrators:

- What data do you already have that points to times and places students persistently misbehave?
- What other data can help you identify systemic stressors for students in the structures and routines of the school day?
- Which colleagues and allied professionals, such as occupational therapists, can you invite to the school to help identify opportunities to decrease persistent student misbehaviors?

For Staff:

- Among your students who most often misbehave, which quick fixes are most likely to yield positive results?
- Among your generally compliant students, which adjustments to structures and routines in your room would help them better focus and succeed academically?
- Which teachers in your building might be most amenable to a conversation with you about short-term and long-term fixes that reduce student misbehaviors?

HACK 5

COMBINE COMPLEXITY WITH CONSISTENCY

DETERMINE WHAT MISBEHAVIORS TO UNIFORMLY ADDRESS

Leadership is the job of forging coherence.
— MICHAEL FULLAN, EDUCATION REFORM LEADER AND AUTHOR

THE PROBLEM: PREDICTABLE CONSISTENCY IS LACKING IN ADDRESSING MISBEHAVIORS

HACK 1 DISCUSSED the student behaviors that require an administrative response, meaning that all other student misbehaviors are the responsibility of the staff members working with students—the standard operating manual for most schools. From the moment students arrive until they are dismissed, different staff may ignore, remind, redirect, or impose punishments for the same behaviors. Staff will make those choices thousands of times a year, almost entirely outside of the administration's view, complicating any hope of imposing uniformity through oversight.

That lack of uniformity within a school filled with complex adults and complex students is impossible to overcome completely. Teaching is a profession, not a born instinct, and the daily decisions that keep a class of young people on task are due to the professional skills of the adults who best know that group of students in the ever-evolving moment. The requirements of the curriculum, coupled with the unique groups of students, demand that teachers continuously recalibrate what can be accomplished on a given day without the teacher becoming rigidly demanding or irresponsibly lenient.

COMPLIANCE WITH TOP-DOWN UNIFORM DEMANDS CAN BECOME TOXIC WHEN IT PREVENTS PERSONALIZED LEARNING AND IN-THE-MOMENT PROBLEM-SOLVING FOR THE GOOD OF THE STUDENTS.

Clearly, that range of scenarios is problematic when we seek to establish norms that can be supported, observed, and assessed—for students and staff alike. For instance, students who have been identified as misbehaving often say, "That's not fair. I wasn't the only one!" I certainly have heard that from many students—and they were often correct. Perhaps just before that student misbehaved, I had reached an emotional limit of tolerance for off-task behavior. Perhaps I had let some behaviors go too far that day, hoping the class could settle down without a strong display of displeasure from me. But there are always students who cannot read an adult's emotional tenor—and too often, they are the ones to transgress and receive a punitive response. I then need to invent a consequence that the student must serve because they transgressed, but the consequence is unlikely to teach the student how to discern the next time I have had enough. Nor will my consequence teach them when any other adult in the school has reached their limit of tolerance for the same or similar behavior. We humans are stubbornly and wonderfully diverse creatures.

Establishing norms that are not rigid can become especially problematic, given the different family and cultural backgrounds and expectations that both adults and students bring with them into the building each day. Given such diversity and the history of power and privilege that we rarely acknowledge but nonetheless remain in the mix, a "third rail" of behavioral concern centers on "respect." What one teacher sees as self-advocacy, another will find disrespectful. The volume and level of teasing between students may sound playful to one staff member and disrespectful to another. A student helping a peer with their work may be applauded by one staff member and interpreted by another as cheating. Because such differences in perspective are deeply embedded in personal, family, and cultural assumptions, in the absence of an obvious way to discuss and establish norms, staff cohesion can be seriously damaged.

The inevitable lack of consistency, when unacknowledged and unaddressed, leads to student confusion and misbehavior, unspoken distrust between staff members, occasional conflict among staff members, and administrative difficulty in evaluating teacher accountability and performance. The impulse to impose rigid behavioral norms—no slouching, absolute silence in the halls, teaching bell-to-bell—will be undermined by even the most compliant teachers as they respond to situations that require improvisation, compassion, and intelligence.

Compliance with top-down uniform demands can become toxic when it prevents personalized learning and in-the-moment problem-solving for the good of the students. No wonder many teachers grow suspicious of administrative demands for compliance, and no wonder administrators often see teachers as being unnecessarily resistant to uniform expectations. It is a setup for conflict. Without a plan to hack discipline, the complexity of the system defies a reasonable level of uniformity.

THE HACK: COMBINE COMPLEXITY WITH CONSISTENCY

Uniformity is binary: you do it or you don't do it. At its best, uniformity saves time and energy. That's the inherent beauty of uniformity in organizations—especially those that are structured for it, such as the army. Schools are not that sort of organization. The range of ages, developmental readiness, curricula, goals, and experiences of the people who walk into a school every day demand that schools be far more flexible than the military. Ultimately, that flexibility is our strength as educators when we temper it with a degree of uniformity.

To work well, uniformity within the complexity of a school must be imposed with great tact. When creating a list of student behaviors that everyone always addresses, keep it short enough to be effective, including only what will absolutely help the staff collectively be successful and only what the administration can consistently support. In schools with a wide range of grades, such as a K–8 school, teachers may ignore behaviors in the early grades, whereas the same behavior in a middle school would definitely need to be addressed in the moment. In such situations, uniformity may be confined to grades, reflecting the developmental needs and abilities of those students.

WHAT YOU CAN DO TOMORROW

FOR ADMINISTRATORS:

- **BEGIN THE CONVERSATION.** This step is similar to the activity in Hack 1 to identify the misbehaviors that require administrative attention. Whether via email, a full staff meeting, or smaller meetings in the school, let everyone know that you want to establish clarity about which student misbehaviors require a staff response. Be sure to make abundantly clear that a subsequent step in this process will be to offer a menu of responses that are suitable for the child and the situation; for now, the goal is to agree on which misbehaviors staff *must* respond to.

- **SHARE THE FIRST DRAFT.** Send out a first draft of the behaviors requiring a staff response, and ask for feedback. You may ask grade-level teams, as well as departments or middle school teams, to discuss the list and reply all together. Here is a sample list of student misbehaviors that do not require administrative involvement but must be addressed by staff. This list is not meant to be definitive or to apply to all schools—each school must craft its own list:
    - interrupting instruction and class focus
    - ignoring a direct request
    - yelling
    - leaving a mess for others to clean up
    - running in the hall
    - tardiness to class
    - technology infraction
    - non-abusive swearing

- **GET FEEDBACK ON YOUR NONNEGOTIABLES.** In a school with a Hacking Discipline Committee, the committee will be the primary driving force in developing drafts, leading to a final list. Within that committee, administrators can also suggest the nonnegotiables for them. The committee's response to those nonnegotiables gives administrators a sense of how much pushback or acceptance they will get from the entire staff, allowing the administrators to decide whether they want to spend their political capital on demanding an unpopular item on the list.

FOR STAFF:

- **IDENTIFY THE MISBEHAVIORS YOU WANT TO UNIFORMLY ADDRESS.** In the absence of a schoolwide determination of misbehaviors demanding staff responses, you can establish your own boundaries and rules. Keep the list short; you are making a public commitment to your students to be reliable and predictable–and they will be watching. For instance, rather than listing all the ways students can disrupt the focus of their peers on a lesson, you can simply include "disrupting the lesson."
- **WORK WITHIN YOUR DAILY CAPACITY.** Know your own tolerances and your capacity to be consistent–and don't go beyond them. Developing trust with students is predicated on being reliable and true to your word. For most people, a short list of absolutes they can enforce is more likely to garner trust

and respect than a comprehensive list that cannot be enforced.

- **INCORPORATE STUDENT VOICE.** Just as staff follow-through is more likely when they have a voice in the process, student buy-in increases when they, too, have a voice in the process of developing the class behavior list. That said, teachers can clearly state their nonnegotiables for the final list. When students know that the adults around them have a few nonnegotiables, and when the adults maintain their commitment to those nonnegotiables, students feel safer. Students should see how their input improved the list.
- **REFRAME THE LIST AS POSITIVE BEHAVIORS FOR STUDENTS.** The list of misbehaviors that must be addressed should be easy for staff to remember and communicate to each other (e.g., "yelling" is a one-word message that takes up little space on a form and can be used when an administrator and teacher have limited time to talk). But in working with students, if we want to share a list of classroom rules, reframe the misbehaviors into positive expectations. For example, instead of a classroom rule that says, "No yelling," try "Speak softly." Reminding students what to do is almost always preferable to telling them to stop what they are doing–in times of stress, students truly may not be able to find the behavior that will rescue them from trouble. Our consistent use of positive expectations will direct them to do the right thing.

- **SHARE YOUR OPERATING MANUAL.** Many students will find it helpful if you make explicit not just the behavioral boundaries associated with a lesson but the ways that students can best interact with you (i.e., let them know your operating manual as an adult). Adults are extremely diverse in how we operate; students struggle to read our many styles and beliefs. Making our styles and beliefs clear will increase the likelihood that students will behave better in our presence. You will also be providing them with a rich model of social-emotional learning through your self-awareness, a lesson they may never get so directly delivered and then demonstrated for an entire school year. Here is a list of some components of adult operating manuals that students can appreciate knowing:

Things about you

- How do you and your students earn and keep each other's trust?
- What are your email and texting boundaries and uses?
- What are your nonnegotiables?
- What do you do for fun?
- How do you show students that you care for them? In what ways might your caring be a challenge for some students?
- How strict are you about timekeeping (e.g., does a minute mean sixty seconds for you?)

- What makes you feel happy and cared for?
- How do you self-soothe amid work?
- How long do you take to solidify first impressions?
- What are your personal space boundaries?
- What triggers strong reactions in you?
- What things in class upset you, and why?
- What distracts you?

Things about how you run the class

- How and when can students advocate for their needs?
- How do students gain the floor to speak in class?
- How do you want students to set up a meeting with you?
- How and when can you be interrupted?
- What level of noise do you find acceptable?
- How can students have permission to move about the room or leave the room?
- What can students do when they finish their tasks ahead of others?
- When are there times for students to share their non-academic stories?

A BLUEPRINT FOR FULL IMPLEMENTATION

STEP 1: Develop widespread agreement on misbehaviors that all will address.

A Hacking Discipline Committee is an excellent vehicle to develop a concise list of behaviors that all staff must address. In the absence of such a committee, administrators can circulate drafts of a list as they gather feedback through emails, one-on-one conversations, and discussions with grade-level and department teams. A transparent process that clearly integrates staff voice will be far easier to implement, support, and evaluate.

STEP 2: Accept less than 100 percent agreement.

Ideally, it would be wonderful if an entire staff unconditionally affirmed a list of student misbehaviors that they must address—but I don't expect that to happen, except in the smallest of schools. The strength of a school with a large and diverse staff usually hinders 100 percent consensus. I have learned that if a vast majority of the staff affirm a plan, their collective wisdom is likely worth following. I will then seek out the staff who did not affirm the plan and let them know that when they find themselves in the vast majority in the future, they, too, will get to rule the day. Engaging in such conversations within a transparent process increases the chance that those not in full agreement will still follow the plan for the sake of staff unity.

> **A HACKING DISCIPLINE COMMITTEE IS AN EXCELLENT VEHICLE TO DEVELOP A CONCISE LIST OF BEHAVIORS THAT ALL STAFF MUST ADDRESS.**

STEP 3: Assure staff they will have needed autonomy.

One barrier in many schools when developing such a list of misbehaviors is that many staff, even if they agree that the list is right for their school, may be worried that they will have to apply uniform consequences. Staff need to hear that identifying the behaviors to be consistently addressed does not mean they are locked into rigid responses. Just as in Hack 2, where a menu of administrative responses to student misbehavior allows for professional discretion, the same will be true for staff. Hack 6 will explore staff responses to student misbehavior. For a list of staff responses to be effective, the first step will be to agree on the misbehaviors that educators must address.

STEP 4: Provide professional development on countertransference.

Countertransference is a term from the world of therapy—basically, it means that we bring our personal histories, hopes, fears, and triggers into all our interactions with students. For instance, there have been students whom I did not like. I struggled to provide them with the warmth and enthusiasm I expected to give to all my students. Surprisingly, my teaching partner across the hall often loved those students! Those students triggered a personal and deep response in me through no fault of their own. Subsequently, my teaching partner and I reacted to those students differently.

In writing the prior paragraph, I purposely used the phrase "did not like" to describe those students. I did so because countertransference at that level is inevitable; we are not going to like every student equally. Our countertransference becomes problematic when we cannot talk about it, leaving us professionally vulnerable to reacting to the transgressions of some students while overlooking the same behaviors in their peers. Honoring that we are professionals in schools means that we meet the challenge of treating every student with equal dignity. They don't have to earn it.

As a school principal, I provided professional development on countertransference; I wanted the entire staff to have a shared language to discuss this inevitable aspect of being human. After the training, I would start a staff meeting by telling a story about my own countertransference—or, in more common language, getting triggered by a student—and what I did in the moment to provide that student with the level of dignity we held as a standard in our school. Perhaps I took three deep breaths or remembered how important it could be in the life of this student for me to remain calm. I wished to normalize with the staff my struggle to hold professional standards. I then asked the staff to share a similar situation in their work with another person. With those partners, the staff then brainstormed ways each of them could manage their countertransference—we all need such a toolkit for this work.

If we ask school staff to develop solid professional relationships with our students and to see the good in all, and in the simplest terms, to love all the students, we will discover the limits of that lofty aspiration. We will confront our countertransference. Hacking school discipline will be more successful when we can talk about and build our collective skills to manage our countertransference.

STEP 5: Describe the components of respect.

Forms of respect are not universal, from requirements or prohibitions on head coverings indoors to the distance people stand apart when they talk. Some children are brought up to speak their truth to adults, while others are expected to bow their heads in silence. Even in schools and communities that, on the surface, appear to be homogeneous, children learn different forms of respect in their homes—as have the adults who work in those schools.

No one likes to be treated disrespectfully—even if that manifests differently from person to person. The misbehavior of certain students can easily trigger countertransference when we feel disrespected—even if the behavior was unintentional. We can forget in those moments that they are students still learning to manage the complexity of this world.

If a staff member proposes adding a respect-related misbehavior to the list (such as "Does not speak respectfully"), ask the staff to identify the components of respect in that context. Seek concrete and observable behaviors, not implicit or indefinable ones. We are far more likely to reach staff consensus when we identify specific behaviors than when we require "respect." For instance, "Does not speak respectfully" might turn out to be "Speaks far louder than is needed to be heard" or "Rolls eyes."

These steps and the plan for full implementation correspond with the January–February sample schedule in Hack 1.

OVERCOMING PUSHBACK

Identifying when teachers must respond to student misbehaviors can be experienced as a big loss of the professional autonomy they have had in their classrooms. The process of publicly working through drafts of the list can diminish some concerns, as will limiting the list to what most all would agree to. Nonetheless, creating uniformity where there has largely been complete autonomy may require additional conversation and assurances.

I want to address behaviors that are not on the list. Staff should always address their concerns with students versus ignoring problematic behaviors. Administration should back a teacher's efforts to maintain safety and a calm environment. The learning opportunity for the adults involved will be in reviewing how that misbehavior was addressed. Above all, we should ask ourselves if our responses were reasonable, respectful, and related.

If I always address every behavior on the list, I won't have time to do anything else. First, the staff member has to try working with the list and then report back on the impact. The test runs conducted by their peers have been analyzed to reduce the likelihood that the list of misbehaviors presents an undue burden. If the staff member reports back that they followed the list and their concern remains, they may need support to look at structures and routines in their classroom or office (as in Hack 4) that need addressing. As well, staff members may need to hear multiple times that their job does include fully focusing on the misbehaviors on the list—at times more than on their lesson plans.

Students know when they are being disrespectful. I want to use that word when I correct them. Begin responding by agreeing that no one should be treated disrespectfully. However, there is no way to know what all students understand about respect and disrespect. For a student who does not know what a staff member is referring to, and without an explanation, they are now even more vulnerable to further trouble. However, a small bit of rephrasing can turn such a situation into a teachable moment and improve the adult-student relationship. Instead of an overly broad assumption about respect, the adult clarifies their definition of respect in the moment (as they might do in their "operating manual"). For example, they may say, "I find it disrespectful when you are so loud. I'd like you to lower your voice." Give staff members opportunities to identify the elements of respect they bring to work and time to practice the phrasing modeled here.

THE HACK IN ACTION

The main agenda item for the next meeting of the Hacking Discipline Committee was to review staff feedback about student misbehaviors that needed to be uniformly addressed by all staff. Principal Anna disseminated a first draft. There had been lively conversations throughout the building. Committee members shared proposed additions to the list, and some offered pointed criticism they had heard regarding items on the first draft.

Ms. R, the guidance counselor, spoke up first. "The conversations about respect were really interesting!" she said. "The issue came up so often, especially from the middle school teachers. That makes sense. Developmentally, kids in middle school are supposed to test rules. It's a time in life when they are trying to figure out what adults really care about—and also, they are dealing with all sorts of new feelings they don't always express … respectfully. I don't think we can get consensus—and I know consensus doesn't have to be absolutely 100 percent—but I think people are happy that we are going to provide guidance on this."

"I have to tell you," said Ms. F, the pre-K/grade 1 teacher on the committee, "some of our littlest students sound like those teenagers! You should hear the things they say!" Everyone laughed.

Anna asked, "Ms. F, what do you do when those little ones speak like that? I am assuming you don't punish them."

"Oh no," Ms. F said. "We pull them aside and tell them how to talk nicer, and then we ask them to say what they said again, but this time nicely."

"Sometimes, I think the kindergarten model would work well in every grade. Time for naps, snacks …" Anna mused.

Suddenly, Mr. D, the industrial arts teacher, got up from his seat and lay down dramatically in the middle of the floor. He looked at all the committee members. "How would you like to come into my shop and see me teaching like this? Or walk into a bakery and see the staff sitting on the floor? That wouldn't be okay. Look, we are teaching kids in school how to act respectfully in the real world. It's not kindergarten out there. They must learn to sit at desks and face the person talking to them. That's the real world of work."

"Mr. D," said AP Maria, "I am glad you don't let students lie on the floor in your shop."

"But artists sit and stand and lie down in all sorts of ways to do their jobs," said Ms. V, the art teacher.

"And in the library, we have big beanbags for kids to snuggle up in when they read," said Ms. K, the librarian.

"And in kindergarten, I don't worry about what job they will have," said Ms. F. "I don't even know what types of jobs will be available in twenty years."

Principal Anna spoke up. "Mr. D, thanks for raising our awareness of your concern. Here is what I am taking from this conversation and how I want us to move forward: clearly, the rules for where and how students can sit, stand, and lie down in our classrooms are not going to be uniform across the school. I will assume the lack of consensus on this committee is what we would hear if we surveyed the entire staff. That said, what school leadership can expect is that every teacher is clear about such boundaries in their rooms. Mr. D, am I right to assume that the rules for how to sit and stand around the equipment in your room will absolutely be enforced every day, no matter who the student is?"

"Absolutely!" said Mr. D as he got back to his chair.

Anna's voice echoed Mr. D's: "That level of absolute certainty must be behind every item we put up on this list of student misbehaviors to address. Let's hear what we've got."

"Before we begin that," said Mr. L, the veteran social studies chair, giving everyone a long look, "I just want to say that I thought I would be the strictest person on the committee—but I do let students sit however they want—including on the floor—when we are reading all together."

"Ah, Mr. L, you're getting soft," joked Ms. K, the librarian.

By the end of the month, after circulating two more drafts among the staff, Anna approved a short and clear list of student misbehaviors that staff will always address, to be piloted later in the year. But first, the committee had to turn their attention to the ways staff would be supported and expected to address those behaviors.

The misbehaviors on the list in Hack 5 are the ones that every adult must address—the list is not comprehensive to all the misbehaviors seen in schools. Given the incredibly wide range of student misbehaviors throughout the year and the varied contexts in which staff work with students exhibiting those behaviors—gym, cafeteria, science lab, hallways, counseling office, and classrooms—adults must exercise their professional autonomy to maintain a safe learning environment.

For Administrators:

- Which staff members may need one-on-one conversations to understand this step in hacking discipline?
- What student behaviors do you currently label as disrespectful that need to be more clearly described?
- What is in your toolkit to manage countertransference when a student is misbehaving?

For Staff:

- Which of the behaviors on the schoolwide list will you find most challenging to address?
- Which of your current students do you most often ignore when they misbehave?
- What are the most important elements of your "operating manual" for students to know in order to prompt their good behavior?

HACK 6

TEACH VERSUS PUNISH

ORGANIZE A TOOLKIT OF STAFF RESPONSES

We need to understand the difference between discipline and punishment. Punishment is what you do to someone; discipline is what you do for someone.

— ZIG ZIGLAR, SALESMAN AND AUTHOR

THE PROBLEM: WITHOUT TOOLS AND SUPPORT, DISCIPLINE CAN STILL BE PUNITIVE

THE RANGE OF responsibilities teachers are expected to fulfill each hour is enormous. The list often includes maintaining a physically safe classroom, organizing supplies for the lesson at hand, greeting every child, taking attendance and sharing announcements, guiding all the students through the many steps of the lesson, assessing the progress of each child moment to moment, providing spontaneous solutions to the challenges any student may suddenly encounter, monitoring the entire class, considering whether the questions students are asking deepen or distract from the instructional goals of the lesson and if there is time enough to answer those questions, attending to the many accommodations and modifications for students with individualized learning plans and 504 plans, providing time for students to understand their homework, ensuring all the students clean up their areas and gather all their belongings before they transition to their next activity or teacher … and, in many cases, far more.

All of those activities do not take into account any student misbehavior, regardless of the cause or the impact of the misbehavior on the learning environment. What is most certain is that teachers do not build into lesson plans time for attending to misbehavior. Sadly, I have heard a teacher say at the end of a challenging day, "Everything would have been fine if the students didn't show up." Students in large groups are inevitably unpredictable in their behavior.

ADDITIONAL STRESS FOR TEACHERS COMES WITH NOTICING IF THEY ARE CONSISTENT AND EQUITABLE IN THEIR REACTIONS TO MISBEHAVIOR.

Often adding to the stress teachers experience is a lack of school-approved options to deal with misbehavior. Is it ever okay in this school to raise one's voice and show frustration? Will that help students understand the interpersonal consequences of their actions in preparation for the larger world? How often is it acceptable to ignore off-task behaviors, such as students talking, staring out the window, or drumming their fingers on a desk? There are so many opportunities to comment on behaviors that a lesson can lose all its momentum. There is no perfect response to everything students do.

Additional stress for teachers comes with noticing if they are consistent and equitable in their reactions to misbehavior. The students have so many different personalities, family cultures, and histories of success and failure. If I individualize my responses, I may be reacting to biases I never even thought I had. I could also be jeopardizing the trust and safety that are so hard to build with some students.

One more stress: What would my supervisors think if they walked into my classroom and didn't approve of my choices in reacting to student misbehavior? Some supervisors seem to be harsher disciplinarians than others. They may not know that I am quietly monitoring a child's off-task behavior because of my history with that child, what happened yesterday in class, and the potential for greater disruption if I react at this moment. I certainly don't want my supervisor to question my classroom management, especially if the off-task behavior unexpectedly becomes contagious and I suddenly have to deal with a bigger problem. The school has offered no guidelines for making these nuanced decisions.

Many teachers feel all those accumulating stressors daily, perhaps more than ever, with pressures to fill historic learning gaps and more recent gaps from the COVID pandemic. The requirements of predetermined curriculum schedules and time-on-task demands do not encourage understanding and settling down misbehaving students. (For more about how educators can overcome challenges, read *Hacking Teacher Burnout* by Amber Harper.)

A traditional and quick option for addressing misbehavior, one that has been practiced in schools for a long, long time, is to threaten or impose punishments: detentions, loss of privileges, extra busywork for homework, and calling the adults at home. These threats are sometimes weighted with shaming by calling out the student in front of their peers or adding checkmarks to the board next to student names. The effectiveness of these steps may be short-lived, but they don't take a lot of time, and the misbehavior was not ignored—the option of punishment is accepted and ordinary in its application.

In the absence of a hacking school discipline initiative, the default to punishment will continue into the next generation.

THE HACK: TEACH VERSUS PUNISH

In Hack 2, administrators, in collaboration with staff, developed a list of administrative responses to student misbehaviors. In this Hack, the administrators and staff learn and apply the five modes of intervention: directing, collaborating, compromising, accommodating, and monitoring. Those modes set the stage for the school to develop a menu of strategies to foster student learning and reparative actions as a replacement for punishments when misbehavior occurs.

The modes of intervention are adapted for schools from the well-known modes of conflict management used in the military, industry, and other organizations. These intervention modes help identify strategies for interrupting misbehaviors and opportunities for applying in-the-moment redirections.

Directing: In certain situations, a staff member needs to be unambiguously simple and clear in telling students what is expected of them immediately (e.g., following the rules during an emergency). Because the rules are nonnegotiable, the staff member directly states the expected behavior: "Right now, you need to be on the right side of the hallway." Telling students what to do is always better than telling them what to stop doing. Due to the immediacy of the moment, failure to comply in such situations can be included in the behaviors that demand administrative involvement. Staff should not find themselves in directing mode most of the time. If staff is directing too often, structural deficits are likely putting unmanageable demands on some students (see Hack 4), leaving staff vulnerable to an overreliance on threats of punishment.

Collaborating: For situations when there is time to build a mutually satisfying solution with a student, collaboration is a great mode. Staff can interrupt misbehavior and engage the student in collaboration by asking, "How can I help you do this task right now?" The root causes of the misbehavior may not take long to uncover, and in that process, solutions may become obvious. For longer conversations, see Curious Conversations in Hack 8, offering a rich opportunity to turn discipline into student self-reflection and commitment.

Compromising: There are often many goals in each moment of a class—from the standard lesson to the social and emotional growth we wish for our students. When we have limited time to engage with students in conversation, the staff can offer a quick bargain to the student, allowing staff to gain traction on one of their priorities while letting go of a lesser one: "If you can regain your focus on the task right now and stay on task for the next five minutes, then I will give you time to read your book instead of you doing so now. Can we agree on that?" Staff often make such bargains with students; knowing this mode is approved makes the decision to compromise less stressful. The staff can also then talk with their peers—and even a supervisor—about how well their compromises are working out versus hiding this practice.

> **KNOWING THAT THE MODES OF INTERVENTION ARE APPROVED BY THE ADMINISTRATION CAN DECREASE STAFF STRESS, INCREASE CREATIVITY WHEN RESPONDING TO MISBEHAVIORS, AND ENCOURAGE PROFESSIONAL CONVERSATIONS ABOUT DISCIPLINE.**

Accommodating: Accommodating is commonly judged as a failure to hold to standards, but in certain situations, it is a reasonable choice: there is limited time, the misbehavior may be escalating, the resources to contain it are few, and the relationship with the student is fragile. The staff can say, "Yes, I will accommodate that request this time." I made a habit of following up with a student I had accommodated by saying, "I decided to accommodate your request yesterday. I want you to know I may never make that decision again. It worked for both of us this time." There is no guarantee that accommodations will impact how the student behaves in the future. We accommodate because it is the best option in that moment to de-escalate and to maintain the learning environment.

Monitoring: Staff do a tremendous amount of monitoring low-level misbehaviors. They assess whether to expend their time and energy to interrupt those behaviors or let them naturally fade away. Monitoring is different than ignoring; monitoring is active and alert to shifts in the behavior of a student and the class as a whole. Often, staff can interrupt low-level misbehaviors by exerting "proximal control"—walking closer and closer to the misbehaving student; the class has not been further distracted, the student's dignity has not been impacted by being called out in front of peers, and the staff has remained calmly in control.

None of the modes are better or worse than the others. They all have efficacy in certain situations. Knowing that the modes of intervention are approved by the administration can decrease staff stress, increase creativity when responding to misbehaviors, and encourage professional conversations about discipline.

WHAT YOU CAN DO TOMORROW

FOR ADMINISTRATORS:

- **DISCUSS THE CONFLICT MODES WITH THE SCHOOL'S LEADERSHIP TEAM.** Staff will need to know there is unity among the leaders as they support teachers in choosing interventions. As the leaders work through concerns and differences they hold and share their own styles and experiences of managing student misbehavior, they will be doing more than developing unity–they will also be rehearsing the types of conversations they will have with staff. They will better understand the nuances of each mode and the decision-making processes that teachers engage with innumerable times every day.

- **IDENTIFY NONNEGOTIABLES.** Within the modes, there may be certain options for addressing misbehavior that the administration will absolutely want teachers to choose from and others that the administration will ban from the list of options (e.g., "That's not how we treat students around here"). Later in this Hack, I encourage administrators to participate in developing drafts of all the specific responses to student misbehaviors that the staff will choose from day to day. Consensus from the administration on their nonnegotiables as those drafts are developed will facilitate an efficient process and lead to a final draft.
- **BE HONEST ABOUT TRUST.** It is said that teachers make a thousand decisions a day as they guide their diverse and ever-developing students through learning experiences in lessons. Much of the time, staff make their pedagogical decisions far from the eyes and ears of school administrators. The same inevitable autonomy is true about discipline decisions, and will continue to be true, as staff address student misbehaviors wherever and whenever they occur.

For some administrators, by identifying behaviors that belong solely to the staff to address, they acknowledge that they must trust the staff to do this work well. That can be a big leap of faith for some administrators. Be as honest as you can about which staff you trust to be wise and equitable in their discipline and which require more support to do the job well and earn your trust–as administrators already do for pedagogical practices. Don't treat all the staff as if they are on the level of the least-skilled professional, which is too often the case in top-down mandates and professional development.

FOR STAFF:

- **CHART THE INTERVENTION MODES YOU USE.** Most staff have used all the intervention modes at some time, but rarely with explicit intention. Moving from implicit to explicit intentions will lead to better decision-making and allow for professional reflection on those decisions. To begin that reflection, think back on the past day or two at school and make a list of the modes of interventions you implemented. Notice your patterns and inclinations. In the coming days, track the intervention modes you use. By simply noticing existing patterns, you can become more flexible in choosing from the five intervention modes.

- **CONSIDER INDIVIDUAL STUDENTS.** Making your own chart of intervention modes you use allows for consideration of beliefs, attitudes, and interactions with particular students. Hack 5 discussed how countertransference can lead us to react differently, and not necessarily effectively, to students presenting the same behaviors. Charting our intervention choices with a particular student provides us with data to consider whether we have become stuck in a repetitive and ineffective mode of intervention.

A BLUEPRINT FOR FULL IMPLEMENTATION

STEP 1: Craft first drafts of a menu to foster student learning and reparations.

The intervention modes provide a framework to interrupt student misbehaviors and offer ways to provide quick redirections. If a student's misbehavior is repetitive or has significantly impacted the learning environment, the staff need to do more than redirect: they need to teach and provide opportunities for reparations versus imposing punishments that rarely teach or repair. It is time to develop a schoolwide menu that teaches and repairs.

A Hacking Discipline Committee is well-positioned to lead this work. Their own experiences with discipline that teaches and repairs can be the starting point of developing a menu of strategies to share with the school. The committee's involvement in this work gives greater assurance that the menu of strategies will be rooted in the daily work of the staff and will also foster greater staff buy-in. In the absence of a Hacking Discipline Committee, the administrators can invite staff members to preview the first draft before they circulate it for wider feedback.

As with the administrators' list of responses to student misbehaviors, the staff responses must be reasonable, respectful, and related. Here is a sample menu of strategies for staff to use that teach and repair. This list is not comprehensive—each school must craft a menu of strategies that meet the needs of its students and can be applied with the available resources. The focus remains to allow the student to be made whole through the process of repairing the harm done and learning alternative ways of coping. This list overlaps significantly with the sample list of strategies for administrators in Hack 2.

Sample list of responses to student misbehavior:

- Speak to each student separately whenever possible; get away from an audience.
- Ask students to demonstrate replacement behavior in the moment (e.g., "Walk back to the pillar and then walk the rest of the way to your class").
- Collaborative Problem-Solving: "Let's make a plan so you can participate in discussions without shouting out."
- Conduct a Curious Conversation, as explained in Hack 8.
- Loss of privileges, with a plan to regain them.
- Apology in writing or in person.
- Sharing with peers what they learned and their plan to do better.
- Peer circle.
- Restitution to fix damage.
- Reflective writing.

- Talk with adults at home.
- Community service in the classroom or elsewhere to balance the harm done when a directly related repair is not possible.
- Develop a Chill-Out Plan, as explained in Hack 8.
- Mediation.
- Refer to administration for repeat offenders (or particularly difficult or awkward situations).

STEP 2: Provide abundant opportunities for staff input.

All the implementations in this Hack rest with the staff, so administrators or the Hacking Discipline Committee should provide abundant opportunities for staff feedback on subsequent drafts of the menu via emails, department meetings, grade-level meetings, or office hours. This open process generates a richer slate of strategies and creates the necessary reflection and conversations that, by themselves, begin to change the culture of punishment to one of learning and reparations.

STEP 3: Develop a long list of reparations.

Some student misbehaviors disrupt the calm business of the day but do not lend themselves to an obvious repair (behaviors such as breaking a piece of recess equipment in frustration). In these cases, the staff can generate a list of reparative options that allow students to be made whole again through giving back to their community. Examples might be straightening the shelving in class or spending time working with the school custodian.

STEP 4: Implement test runs.

If you have a Hacking Discipline Committee, members of the committee can participate in the first test run; the rest of the staff can be informed of this step, further generating interest in the plan. This effort will also add a degree of legitimacy to the process, supporting further schoolwide buy-in. In the absence of a committee, the administration can seek out staff members who will participate in the first test run.

After the first test run, the administration or Hacking Discipline Committee can implement a schoolwide test run for a specific period, such as two months. The administration gathers data on how the menu of strategies has been used and reviews outcomes for individual students, cohorts of students, and the school as a whole. After adjusting the strategies based on the test runs, the menu becomes standardized as part of the school culture, with perhaps a yearly review for notable changes.

For individual staff members: If your school is not currently hacking discipline, you can make a commitment to use the menu of strategies in your own classroom or office. Perhaps you can find peers who are willing to implement test runs with you.

These steps and the plan for full implementation correspond with the February–March sample schedule in Hack 1.

OVERCOMING PUSHBACK

The pattern of shaming and punishment is well-established in schools. The work the administrators do in Hacks 1 and 2, moving their responses from punishment to reparations, will have made an impact on the school community. Changes first modeled by leadership carry much influence, but veteran teachers may still struggle to adjust to the new expectations discussed in this Hack.

I find that threatening students with detentions and other punishments works just fine. Be sure to first appreciate the work of teachers who have their own approach to discipline. They have probably developed a comfortable practice over many years without a lot of information or support. Without realizing it, they have likely been using means other than threats of punishment to address student misbehavior, such as proximal control, monitoring, collaborating, or expecting students to replace misbehavior in the moment with more acceptable behavior. Ask them to keep track of their choices for a week. Bringing their decision-making to a conscious level will increase the potential for them to consider using more of the nonpunitive responses that are already in their practices.

I don't have time to do this. Teachers have much to do, and few ever complete all of their tasks on a given day—but the claim of "lack of time" is also a way to deflect finding the time or resetting priorities. On their own or with the support of peers and administrators, teachers can share their priority list to learn ways to reorder those priorities to make time for this important schoolwide effort. Teachers can seek an extended deadline to implement this change, or they can seek administrative support to fulfill the task if they are truly having trouble finding the time to work with the menu of strategies. Administrators can remind the staff that they will be collecting feedback on the hacking discipline efforts from the entire staff; if there is widespread difficulty in implementing the plans, the administration will adjust. That feedback will hopefully reveal that staff is ultimately spending less time responding to student misbehaviors because they are making plans with students to avoid a repeat of the misbehavior.

Students need to know the consequences of their actions. Consequences and punishments are not synonymous. Students need to know that there will always be consequences for their actions. Consequences have not disappeared! The work of hacking discipline is embedded in providing staff with an array of consequences, rather than punishments, that can decrease the likelihood of repeat misbehaviors. A consequence, such as detention, is not effective if it does not teach new behaviors or allow the student to repair the harm done. The outcome of hacking discipline—the consequence—is a student who is less likely to misbehave again.

It was better in the old days when we could easily suspend students. It wasn't better in the old days. Students dropped out at rates over five times what is now the norm. The number of dropouts for minority students, who received a disproportionate number of suspensions, was significantly greater than for students of privilege. In the old days, schools absolutely replicated the inequalities in society at large rather than fulfilling the hope of helping all students meet their potential. Suspensions, exclusions, shaming, and rigid punishments were among the least effective practices in the old days.

THE HACK IN ACTION

"My dear committee members, what have you all discovered this week, charting which intervention modes you used?" asked Principal Anna, opening the Hacking Discipline Committee meeting. "Maria and I have been looking over your charts and adding up what you all have done, but I'm more interested now in what you discovered for yourselves since we will be asking the rest of the staff to do their own charting next week."

"Well, it was quite an eye-opener for me," said Mr. D, the vocational teacher. "Everyone around here knows I run a tight shop. There are rules, and you better not break them. I don't compromise, and I certainly don't accommodate any nonsense—or you'll be spending a couple of lunchtimes with me, sweeping up the room and straightening the shelves."

"Send those kids to my kindergarten class," Ms. F interrupted. "I've got lots of shelves every day that I have to straighten up!"

"Let me say," Anna added, "we've come a long way as a team. Many of you had never talked with each other before. Okay, Mr. D, what about those messy shelves of yours?"

"Hah, very funny," replied Mr. D dryly. "What I was wanting to tell you is that it turns out I compromised and accommodated a bunch of times. Nothing big or serious, mind you, but the students are always asking me if they can do things or not do things—like take a break to look out the window—and of course, it depends on the kid and the day and what's going on, but yeah, I was compromising and accommodating a lot. You've got to do that just to keep everything running smoothly."

Around the table, many people nodded in agreement.

"Well, I had quite the opposite experience," said Ms. K, the librarian. "Turns out I'm a bit of a dictator. I was telling students all day what to do and what not to do."

Once again, people nodded, and AP Maria chimed in. "This is why I am excited about getting to this stage of hacking discipline! You won't believe it, but it's true: when I added up the numbers from your charts, there was a little more 'monitoring' than anything else, just ahead of 'directing'—as we all might have predicted—but the other modes were all close! I'm in classes around the school a lot, and I've seen you all using those modes all the time! Anna and I want to send these summaries out to the staff. We'd also like to put all your names on the bottom so the school will know who was part of this test run, but I won't say what anyone's specific data was."

"Good," Mr. D said. "I don't want my reputation as a disciplinarian damaged. Just kidding. You can let everyone know what a softie I've become from sitting on this committee."

"This is all good," Anna said. "You all are helping to normalize the entire hacking process. I think the work we did in the beginning when the main office stopped being seen as only rigid disciplinarians has shifted some of the notions of what discipline can be."

"Not just that," added Mr. L, the veteran social studies department chair, "but you began to communicate with us what you did with the students you disciplined and what we could do based on what you did. That was a game-changer for me."

"Thank you for saying that," Anna answered. "Your participation and support here have assured me that we are on the right track. Thanks to all of you. We have another big job ahead, and that is to do a test run on the menu of strategies that we have been working on for teaching better behaviors and making reparations. We've gotten good feedback from the staff who responded to the first couple of drafts. I am sure they will be looking forward to hearing your experiences in working through the strategies for learning and reparations. That might be the biggest ask we are making in this hacking discipline work: asking everyone to move away from using threats of punishment as their first tool."

"I have a hunch," said Mr. P, the physical education teacher, "that lots of people already do more than threaten students with punishment. Sort of like the data we got from charting the modes of intervention. I think we'll be surprised by all that the teachers do now to discipline students that no one has ever charted. That will definitely be true for me. All the schools I worked in during my training charted only the punishments, so nothing else staff had been doing got headlines."

Everyone around the table quietly pondered Mr. P's prediction.

Ms. R, the guidance director, broke the silence. "I've been thinking," she said, "that we should change our name from the 'Hacking Discipline Committee' to the 'Teaching Better Behaviors Committee.' Sounds more like what we are doing."

The word *discipline* is strongly associated with punishment, in that, a teacher who is considered a strong disciplinarian is rarely known to compromise when necessary or to support a student making reparations instead of serving a silent detention. Fully embracing teaching versus punishing develops a culture that recognizes the potential for growth in every student. Providing options for responding to student misbehaviors can unleash all the creativity of a school community—creativity that may have always been there, operating under the radar in a dominant culture of threats and punishment.

For Administrators:

- Which staff members may need one-on-one conversations to understand teaching versus punishing?
- Which modes of intervention would you like to explore more in your own practice?
- Which specific strategies for teaching and reparations do you most want to support becoming norms in your school, and how can you facilitate that happening?

For Staff:

- Which mode(s) of intervention would you like to focus on more in your work?
- Which of your current students may benefit the most from opportunities to repair the harm done by their misbehavior?
- What can be on your list of reparative actions your students can take in your classroom when the harm of their misbehavior cannot directly be repaired?

HACK 7

LEAVE NO STAFF BEHIND

SHARE THE STORIES THAT GAIN STAFF BUY-IN

People recall information more easily when it is shared via stories than when people are given facts alone.
— TIFFANY MANUEL, SOCIAL CHANGE AUTHOR

THE PROBLEM: STAFF DON'T TRUST PLANS IMPOSED ON THEM

HACK 2 IDENTIFIED the stress many administrators experience as the ultimate disciplinarians in schools that have never been structured or resourced to leave no child behind. Schools that hack discipline will reduce that stress on administrators, who will be operating within more structured and flexible guidelines while effectively communicating and collaborating with the staff.

Of course, the historic failures of our schools weigh heavily on the teaching staff, who are responsible for the daily implementation of almost every innovation to address the embedded dysfunctions and inequities of our educational system.

The teachers are a highly educated group. They have intimate and detailed knowledge of the strengths and weaknesses of their workplace to put the latest innovation into practice. They are also near the bottom of the hierarchy of decision-makers, descending from national boards to state educational departments to local school committees to their own administrative team. Their wisdom and input can be (and often are) routinely marginalized at any rung above them in the hierarchy—and their capacity to take on new initiatives will be part of their job-performance evaluation.

In a fashion, every innovation demanded of the staff asks them to temporarily experience incompetence and take a leap of faith that this innovation will really work. Teachers have earned the right to be wary of one more innovation. They will reflexively raise doubts. They will reasonably demand some proof that what administrators ask of them is worth the extra hours they will put in, after school and on weekends, to get up to speed. Their resistance is not without merit.

THE STORIES OF THOSE WHO VOLUNTEERED FOR TEST RUNS SHOULD INCLUDE STATISTICS ABOUT THE DECREASE IN REPEAT MISBEHAVIORS AND IN THE NUMBER OF STUDENTS SENT TO THE MAIN OFFICE.

All the prior hacks in this book, whether with or without a Hacking Discipline Committee, have in their design strategies to assuage staff doubts. Hopefully, most of the staff has been engaged in reading and commenting on the drafts, participated in test runs, or heard the experiences of their trusted peers who engaged in test runs. The stage is set to present to the school community the summary of all the prior hacks and the plan for full-scale implementation.

It's time to hack gaining staff buy-in.

THE HACK: LEAVE NO STAFF BEHIND

People buy into a significant change most easily when they already have a level of competency and that level of competency is appreciated. The same is true for the collective competency of an entire staff. Even before the prior hacks in this book were implemented, staff members were probably practicing their own versions of restorative discipline. By identifying the current skills demonstrated by the staff to hack discipline, a seemingly impossible task becomes a manageable one, backed up by a plan fully endorsed by leadership.

Tell stories about the school's current competencies. Recap all the hacking work done up until this point. This is an opportunity to publicly thank all the staff who gave feedback on drafts of lists and procedures and piloted test runs. Even if the school has been diligent in keeping the process transparent, reminding everyone that this process has benefited from diverse voices will distinguish the process from far too many prior top-down directives. Staff need to know that many staff members have had their hands in crafting the plan.

Leaders gain buy-in from inspiring stories *and* a few well-chosen data points. Many staff members want to know that in the administration's excitement to carry out this initiative, they are also firmly rooted in numbers and facts. The stories of those who volunteered for test runs should include statistics about the decrease in repeat misbehaviors and in the number of students sent to the main office. You don't need a lot of data that can drain the room of energy. Pick a small number of data and stories as examples of what has already been accomplished and, therefore, what else can be accomplished. More important for buy-in than the statistics of the problems of the past are the statistics of positive change from the test runs and the schools that have implemented similar hacks.

In Hack 1, the administration presented staff with a timeline for developing the hacking discipline plan. Now, the administration can present the timeline for the schoolwide adoption of hacking discipline. They can preview the plans for training and ongoing support. Staff need to hear that they do not have to be competent from day one and that they will be supported to reach competency.

If a Hacking Discipline Committee or several staff members have contributed consistently to the process, they should lead staff presentations. By putting the spotlight on the staff, the presentation plan can be separated from the risk of unearthing old complaints about systemic inertia. *The plan is not a referendum on the school's administration.*

The administration should attend the presentation to communicate their enthusiasm and support, field questions, and be available to provide specific information at their disposal. The administration must affirm that they will bring their full weight to the hacking discipline plan. Staff buy-in depends on administrative commitment to follow through until the change is rooted in the school culture. This is no time to deny administrative power; in a system as complex as a school, staff need to know that those with their hands on the gears of the school's operations are ready to apply their muscle. The presentation is about "all of us," leaving no staff behind.

WHAT YOU CAN DO TOMORROW

FOR ADMINISTRATORS AND STAFF:

- **BE SURE YOU ARE READY TO PRESENT.** At various stages in the school year, leaders are so pressed for time, with so many agendas to complete, that they can rush to check one more item off their list. Before committing to presenting the hacking discipline plan to the entire staff, make sure you can dedicate sufficient time to do it well.

- **SUMMARIZE THE TEST RUNS.** Choose the stories that have the most impact. This is an opportunity to give information in the form of stories, inspire optimism, and reinforce the careful and inclusive process leading to the presentation. In particular, stories of students who have responded positively to the new system are always inspiring.
- **FIND YOUR EXEMPLARS.** Ahead of time, check in with specific staff members, asking them for their permission to publicly appreciate their contributions to the plan. Ask faculty members who participated in the test runs to present. Encourage them to speak briefly about their experiences. Since many staff members don't like to speak in public, offer them a short outline, such as: 1) This is what I experimented with: ________; 2) I learned that: ________; and 3) What I want to keep doing next year is ________.
- **CHOOSE THE MOST COMPELLING DATA.** Identify the data that best illustrates the efficacy of buying into the hacking discipline plan. Focus far more data on the solutions than on the old problems. Find staff members who have stories that illustrate the movement from data to practice.
- **LET FACULTY LEAD.** Secure the assistance of faculty or the Hacking Discipline Committee members

who will take part in the presentation. The most powerful presentation of a hacking discipline plan will be organized and delivered by the committee members. The school leaders can prepare their portion of the presentation and focus on their responsibilities to provide resources and support. If there is no committee, have a planning meeting with those who can participate in the presentation. When possible, ask a veteran teacher who is widely respected to play a prominent role, which can include introducing the presentation and chairing the meeting.

A BLUEPRINT FOR FULL IMPLEMENTATION

Here's an all-too-common scenario: school leaders present an innovation, such as the well-thought-out hacking discipline plan, at a staff meeting. Suddenly, teachers share a barrage of questions and critical comments. The leaders may anticipate the usual critics, but on any day, they can be surprised by the other teachers who join in this public gauntlet of analysis. Some leaders will then shy away from sharing ideas, retreating into silence. Some leaders will decide to work among themselves to hatch all the plans, further alienating the staff. Others will listen with increasing dismay to the staff's reactions and stubbornly say, "I'm doing it anyway."

The problem is that the leaders don't know if a comment or question is because the staff member hates the idea and has every intention of sabotaging it, likes the idea with some reservations, or has some thoughtful advice to offer. Without knowing the intention behind the speaker's words, it can all sound like intransigence and obstruction. Even when a Hacking Discipline Committee is the primary presenter of a plan, questions and concerns inevitably arise.

Here is one protocol to raise staff reactions to a higher level of communication. When you open up the floor for commentary and questions after airing a proposal, ask people to preface their remarks by going in order through these four steps.

STEP 1: I am glad we have this plan.

This opening gives permission to speak for those who may think silence is agreement. Also, for the hacking discipline plan to work, the staff need to hear and feel the affirmation from their peers. Large-scale buy-in, expressed in public, provides the energy to maintain the school's commitment to the future of this innovation.

STEP 2: I am in favor of the idea, and I have a concern about a detail.

Many staff members have an astounding attention to detail. Once they identify a small concern, they feel a responsibility to pass it along—not as a criticism but as a form of support. They want leadership to get this right. By identifying their intention, these staff members will no longer be swirled up in an undifferentiated wave of questioning. Their contributions will be clear and now will be welcomed. They are pushing the plan forward.

STEP 3: I like the idea, but I have a significant concern, and if it is not addressed, I can't back the proposal.

What might look like a comprehensive hacking discipline plan in the principal's office can seem daunting to the teachers in their daily labors. They truly may see a fatal flaw, perhaps an implementation landmine, that needs to be addressed. These staff members are not asking leadership to abandon hacking discipline. In fact, by identifying their intention in raising concerns, they are acting responsibly. The difficulty here is that leadership or the Hacking Discipline Committee may not be able to address the concern in the moment. Leadership needs to say, "Got it. We will look again at the plan to see what we can do about those lines coming in from recess. That is a problem spot. Thanks." Always thank teachers who can identify their intentions in the interest of a better plan.

STEP 4: I do not like this plan at all.

In a diverse and complex school culture, few plans will meet everyone's expectations and demands. If you find a large portion of the staff prefacing their remarks at Step 4, it is likely the plan is critically flawed or the presentation did not reflect the actual workings of the hacking discipline innovation. With a strong Hacking Discipline Committee that has been fully involved in the drafts, test runs, and presentation, fewer people will be speaking in Step 4, and the truly small fraction of stubborn and resistant staff members will no longer look as if they are leading the charge. They are outliers. Politically, their concerns and fears need to be addressed, but not at the larger meeting.

These steps and the plan for full implementation correspond with the March–April sample schedule in Hack 1.

OVERCOMING PUSHBACK

Students outnumber staff by the hundreds (and even thousands) in most schools. Should most of those students rebel from the burden of complying with their daily regimentation, the lack of autonomy, and the relentlessness of the curriculum, the adults would be helpless to stop them. That fear of chaos, sparked by even a fraction of the student body, explains why some staff will find it so hard to move away from traditional discipline rooted in threats and punishments.

We still don't have enough data to prove the change will be better. Be ready with your data. The full faculty presentation shared only a few significant numbers, mostly focused on how improvements were already gaining traction. Offer to share all the data on the incidence of chronic misbehaviors, perhaps going back a few years. Underscore the fact that the culture of threats and punishments was having no impact on these misbehaviors and that the school already has data on its ability to do better. In the end, the staff person may need to hear clearly, "We are not going back."

We're not ready for such a big change. Unpack what the person means by "big." Some staff will project their concerns that they will feel incompetent with the change by generalizing those concerns to the entire school. Ask the person, "What will be hard *for you* to change?" All of their concerns, from training to follow-through on community service, should be addressed in the implementation plan. If they identify a concern not in the plan, thank them for doing so.

Unintended consequences always pop up after making a change. That is an absolutely true statement—though not a reason to avoid change. We could make a long list of historic changes schools made to improve the outcomes for students and the conditions for staff: central heating, special education services, equal access to all courses for girls, hiring reading specialists, and posting homework online. All of these came with unintended consequences. As well, the plans for hacking discipline discussed in Hack 10 will include monitoring the system for those inevitable unintended consequences.

THE HACK IN ACTION

Principal Anna started the committee meeting by announcing that she and AP Maria were able to secure one full staff meeting in the spring dedicated to a big presentation from the Hacking Discipline Committee. There was a smattering of applause and snapping fingers. Everyone knew that Anna and Maria had done a lot of negotiating and compromising and had spent a lot of their political capital with the superintendent and curriculum directors, whose own agendas could dominate every school meeting.

"Thanks for that bit of appreciation," Anna said. "This is about all of us, isn't it? When I was pushing hard to protect the staff meeting for our presentation, I felt all of you in the room with me. I've realized how often, as a principal, I have had to operate largely from my own perspective. It's so much better to have a staff team at my back, with all your stories and passions informing me and inspiring me."

After a brief pause, she said, "Today, we will be organizing the presentation. We won't do all the work here. We'll identify what we must do to develop a great presentation, divide up that work among us, and get started on those tasks. Before we leave today, we'll set deadlines to get those tasks done. Maria and I need time to put together the slide deck for the presentation and set the order of speakers."

Maria spoke up. "Anna and I were thinking that one of you should co-chair the meeting with us. We'll introduce and close the presentation, but maybe in between that, one of you could take over the podium. The bulk of this presentation should come from you all."

"I'd be interested in co-chairing," said Mr. P, the physical education teacher.

"Oh, I think that would be great," Maria immediately responded. "You work with more of the students than almost anyone. You know a lot of the newer and younger staff whose enthusiasm, like yours, can make a big difference in this work."

Heads were nodding around the room. Through the course of their meetings, most committee members had made it clear that public speaking was not a task they did easily. They had joked that a hidden agenda for participation on the committee was to urge them to talk in public, whether to a department, the parent organization, or the school board.

In contrast to his unconfident peers, Mr. P was a natural at the microphone. His talk to the parent organization one afternoon in the spring was funny and passionate and well organized. In his first year at the school, he built good relationships with the lunch staff, the maintenance crew, and the bus drivers. Many at the table were already imagining the energy he would bring to the presentation. He was an obvious choice.

Then Mr. L, the veteran social studies department chair, raised his hand. He took a slow look around the table. "With all due respect to Mr. P, with whom I have shared a few good laughs when we were on lunch duty this spring, I want to make a counter-suggestion." He turned to Anna. "I say this with all due respect to our principal, whom I have worked with for many years. I knew she was good, but being on this committee has made me understand even more all she has to do to make this school function as well as it does. I don't think Anna or Maria should be up on the podium at all for this presentation." He looked once again around the table. "I think those of us who are not administrators should run the entire presentation for the staff." He paused one more time. "And I think I should chair that meeting."

Everyone on the committee, in their own way, did a double take. Then Ms. K, the librarian, spoke up. "Mr. L," she said, "you never cease to amaze me. I was surprised you joined this committee in the first place. And then you've sort of become a convert to our mission here, even though now I understand that you always did a lot of what we are asking everyone to do with their students. But, wow, you have to tell us more."

Before he could speak, Mr. P, the physical education teacher, said, "I get it. Mr. L, you'll be great. I can't believe I didn't think of it. Yeah, it has to be you!"

"Well," Mr. L sighed, "it doesn't have to be me. But it should be. Let me explain my thinking. First, I've been in this school a long time, and we've made many changes, even before Anna was principal, but maybe none as big as this one, because every staff member has to be on board. Asking people to change how they discipline misbehavior may be as hard as asking people to change what they eat."

"People are suspicious of administrators. As I said, I have learned a lot about what it takes to run a school by sitting in these meetings, but most staff members still have no idea. If Anna and Maria run the presentation, half the staff will push back simply because the ideas are coming from them. But they won't push back if we are in charge and if the ideas come from us."

Anna said, "I've been thinking and worrying about the same thing. All of you have done the work. Maria and I have done our parts, but the rest has been yours, from brainstorming to sharing stories to the test runs and all the conversations in your grade-level and department meetings. It didn't sound right for me to oversee the staff presentation—and yes, it is true that I get pushback simply for being the principal. I am used to it, but this meeting doesn't need to be about me at all. I agree."

"That also explains why I want to chair the presentation," Mr. L said. "Not that I am immune from pushback, but the people who I fear will make or break our discipline hack will be the veteran staff. If they don't buy in, and if they start raising all sorts of concerns because that's the role veterans are supposed to play on the staff, we will lose momentum. And they may instill doubts in the younger staff. If I chair the meeting and I affirm the process we followed—and I say I am on board—well, that's another role a veteran staff person can play in this school. I think I am the best one here to do that."

"I agree," said Ms. R, the guidance director. "Everyone respects Mr. L. We don't hear students complaining about him in our department. He's an icon in the school. Let's use him."

"Yes!" said Mr. P. "How about this idea? What if I co-chair the meeting with him? Then we have one of us who can influence the veterans, and I have my influence with the newer staff. And it would be an honor for me to be up there with Mr. L."

"That would be very nice," said Mr. L. "We would make a good team."

"Hold on a second," said Ms. K, the librarian. "Two-thirds of the staff in this school are women, and for many of us, it's been great to watch Anna and Maria be in charge. This is not a time to ignore the importance of women leaders when we are asking all staff to buy in. And we know the history in this country of students of color getting harsher discipline. We need someone who looks like them up on the podium. I'd like to be on that presentation team."

STAFF NEED BOTH A SOLID IMPLEMENTATION PLAN AND THEIR OWN PONDERING PROCESS TO REACH BUY-IN.

The committee quickly reached a consensus on Ms. K's proposal. They subsequently divided up responsibilities for the presentation and began work on those tasks.

Anna closed the meeting by saying, "Going back to Mr. L's analogy of asking the staff to change the food they eat, I've often thought that our discipline hacks were like a healthier and better-tasting drink than the sweet, processed sodas many people are used to, which are analogous to the traditional threat and punishment version of discipline. We have a new and better product to offer: self-control, accountability, and relationships. All this year, we have been offering staff sips of our new drink. We've been test marketing it. Those who have tried our new approach like it. Now we are ready to launch our all-out campaign. And I don't think we could have asked for a better trio of spokespersons to get us started."

School leaders often ponder the need for a big innovation over the course of many weeks, if not months or years. They talk with other leaders, read through the research, and perhaps find time to include community stakeholders in their contemplation. By the time they are ready to present their plan to the staff, they have worked through their doubts, the options, and the potential pitfalls. They may quickly summarize all their considerations for the staff before the big reveal of the plan. In their excitement or when laboring under a deadline, leaders overlook the fact that the staff must work through their own doubts, weigh the options, and imagine potential pitfalls. Staff need both a solid implementation plan and their own pondering process to reach buy-in.

For Administrators:

- For a successful staff buy-in at your school, when do leaders need to be in the lead, and when do they need to step back?
- In your school, what considerations for buy-in from veteran staff are similar to or different from gaining buy-in from newer staff?
- How can you adapt, in your own words and in the culture of your school, the four steps for responding to staff reactions when you make presentations?

For Staff:

- In what ways do you want to know that staff have played a significant role in developing plans for school innovations?
- In what ways are you influenced by stories, and in what ways are you influenced by data?
- In what ways have you seen the four steps for staff reactions to leaders play out in your school?

HACK 8

PREVENT INSTEAD OF INTERVENE

DESIGN DE-ESCALATION PLANS BEFORE THEY'RE NEEDED

It's better to be a warrior in a garden than a gardener in a war.
— MIYAMOTO MUSASHI, JAPANESE PHILOSOPHER

THE PROBLEM: EDUCATORS ARE ENDLESSLY REACTING TO STUDENT MISBEHAVIORS

EVEN TEACHERS WHO are attuned to the mood and attentiveness of a class cannot predict when a given student has had enough. One moment, the day is going as planned, and the next, there is a crisis to contain.

Many students need a reliable set of coping tools to manage all the cognitive, sensory, and emotional demands of school day after day after day. Their feelings are strong, and they are vulnerable to misbehaving, depending on the teacher's rules and temperament. The student may simply look up from their work to scan the room and be told, "Eyes on your paper." The teacher has no idea what is going on for the student. The student has no idea what else to do.

If all goes well, the student will quietly cope without disrupting the learning environment. Most students, most of the time, have the self-control to compartmentalize their concerns and at least make a show of doing the lesson—even if it's far from their best capacity. But typical students will have times when they misbehave in ways that surprise themselves, their peers, and the teacher because they couldn't meet the expectations placed on them in the moment.

Many students face this struggle to cope daily. Most notable in this group are our millions of students with trauma histories. Their experiences have taught them to be hypervigilant about perceived danger, including feeling vulnerable, being called out, or getting punished. Their inner "air raid sirens," warning them of potential trouble, are easily triggered by random classroom events, blocking out their cognitive strengths. Their sirens are louder and last longer than those of many of their peers who haven't experienced the same level of trauma. Despite their academic abilities and motivations to learn, they are at risk of suddenly being overwhelmed in class with no available coping strategies. Often, they don't know what to do to stay out of trouble. They experience a more extreme and scarier version of coping than their peers.

MANY STUDENTS NEED A RELIABLE SET OF COPING TOOLS TO MANAGE ALL THE COGNITIVE, SENSORY, AND EMOTIONAL DEMANDS OF SCHOOL DAY AFTER DAY AFTER DAY.

The structures and routines addressed in Hack 4 will greatly reduce the incidence of misbehaviors caused by systemic dysfunctions. But the inner turmoil that builds into misbehaviors in students will unfortunately remain—and emerge randomly. The teacher is challenged to improvise a course of action that does not draw undue attention to their plight, interrupt the momentum of the lesson for the rest of the class, or shame, threaten, or punish the student.

I've asked hundreds of educators how they manage to step back from feeling overwhelmed. Some need silence and isolation, some listen to music, and many seek out a trusted confidant. A good many choose to clean, some head to the gym, and others practice mindful deep breathing. As adults, we have scores of options to choose from; no one way works for everybody.

I have heard a recurring message from educators: "I don't want to hear advice until I ask for it. And don't try to talk me out of my feelings—really don't do that!" Conversely, no one says, "I like being commanded to sit still in an uncomfortable chair and then being told what I should feel instead of what I actually feel, and as a bonus, getting a lecture about what I did wrong." And yet, that is what we so often do to our students, especially if their misbehaviors disrupt our plans.

I am amazed by our students' faith in adults to help them, given how we often impatiently react to their pain and frustration, to their fight and flight and freezing up, and to the manifestations of their struggles. Perhaps, sadly, some learn that the adults are of limited help when the students don't know how to help themselves.

The problem is not that the students have strong emotions—we can't stop those emotions from developing. Strong emotions are a condition of being a human being, more so in a large institution within which one has little authority. Adults who work in such large organizations, from schools to the military to insurance companies, also feel the periodic rage and despair of not being in control of their workplace; in that way, our students are our peers. The problem is that we have not instituted strategies that help students cope. We are always reacting. It is time to hack extreme or disproportionate reactions.

THE HACK: PREVENT INSTEAD OF INTERVENE

The good news is that we can help students learn to cope with their feelings, communicate with us when they want and need our support during their hard moments, and find again and again the ability to focus on their schoolwork. The key is to prepare them for hard times when they *are not* at their most overwhelmed. As has been said by many with trauma-informed practices, "The top of the emotional escalator is not a teachable moment. At that point, just be safe and chill out."

Adults who drive where winter brings ice and snow understand the need to be safe and chill out from the times our cars skidded on a frozen roadway. We turn the steering wheel this way, then the other way, pump the brakes, stomp the brakes, grimace, and hope the car comes safely to rest before someone, or something, is hurt. When we finally halt—if we are lucky, without having collided with anything—we invariably take a few deep breaths, maybe shut off the car for a minute, and then resume our trip. We are safe, and we take a moment to chill out.

However, what we haven't learned from that experience is how to drive a skidding car. We are just as vulnerable to the next skid, in the exact same condition of panic and powerlessness as every other skid that we have survived. Just as with our students who panic and misbehave, we move on with no more skills to manage the next incident.

For drivers who need to learn to control a car on ice, there are "skid schools" on a frozen tarmac, safe from obstacles and people. With a trainer in the passenger seat, you practice the steering and braking techniques to safely control a skidding car. And then you practice again. You improve your ability to manage the stress of the moment by developing competency through skills and practice.

That's what we can do for students, especially for those who are most at risk of emotionally skidding into fleeing, fighting, or freezing: we give them opportunities to practice gaining control when they are not overwhelmed. We help them develop their set of chill-out tools, we praise them when they practice with us, and we support them in using their chill-out tools in the moment.

Providing these students with the tools to be safe and chill out is as viable as providing different colored pencils for a task. Just as important, these tools are good for every child to have and can be easily implemented by the school staff. We normalize everyone having clear chill-out strategies. Regaining control is teachable. Prevention is better than intervention. Following are more details about two prevention methods: Chill-Out Plans and Curious Conversations.

Prevention Method #1: Chill-Out Plans

Every child chooses three options from a menu of chill-out strategies (see sample list). One option they can do unobtrusively from their seat; one option they can do in another section of the room; another option happens outside of the room, depending on safety or the availability of an adult to monitor the student. A copy of the Chill-Out Plan—with drawings or stickers for our youngest students—stays with the student. Copies of the list are filed in the student database so any adult working with a student can quickly access the plan.

The students are given opportunities to practice their plans once they are developed and then periodically through the year, and they are always praised for working on their plans. The teacher says, "Everyone, it's time to practice the Chill-Out Plan you do in your seat. We'll do this for three minutes. Let's get good at chilling out." This practice strategy is also useful for when a class has become restless or is preparing for a transition.

For students who need extra practice, a teacher, counselor, or any adult who knows the child can initiate a practice session: "Let's pretend for a moment you are upset. What Chill-Out Plan can we do now? I'll stay with you for three minutes to give you practice."

With these plans in place, a student can signal to the adult that they need to use their plan. The adults can also signal to a student to use their Chill-Out Plan when a situation is escalating. Chill-Out Plans are also useful immediately after a crisis and before any analysis, lecturing, or restorative responses are implemented. Most memorably, a teenage student said to me in a tense moment, "Mr. B, can we both just chill out now?"

Sample list of chill-out strategies:

- put head down on desk
- put on noise-reducing headphones
- listen to music with headphones
- doodle/sketch/color
- sit or lie in quiet area
- stand or walk or do movement in designated area
- write in a journal
- use a fidget object
- look out the window
- get a drink of water
- read
- work on a puzzle
- do another academic task
- chores in class: clean, straighten, water plants
- crafts: macramé, knit, sew
- talk with a trusted adult
- help out elsewhere in school

- talk to a sibling in the school
- use the gym
- take a walk

Image 8.1 shows a basic Chill-Out Plan form. Younger students can note their choices with pictures of stickers. Older students can be encouraged to add specific details to address their unique needs.

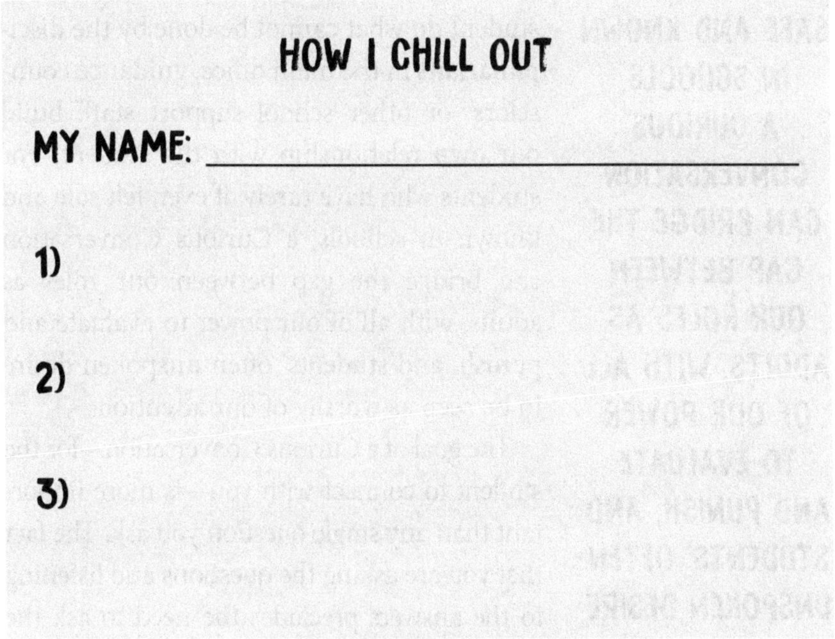
HOW I CHILL OUT

MY NAME: ____________________

1)

2)

3)

Image 8.1

Prevention Method #2: Curious Conversations

The Curious Conversation is a tool that builds trust, student reflection, and emotional growth. While all students would benefit from such an activity, the ones who need it the most, such as the students who chronically upend the class with their impulsive misbehavior, are often the last ones we want to spend more time with. But when we do spend time hearing about their experiences as students and just hearing them without layering on a lesson about how they can improve, we help them change simply by listening to them. In my work with students who have had traumatic lives, many students told me that I was the first teacher who ever asked them some basic questions about what has and hasn't worked for them in classrooms.

FOR STUDENTS WHO HAVE RARELY, IF EVER, FELT SAFE AND KNOWN IN SCHOOLS, A CURIOUS CONVERSATION CAN BRIDGE THE GAP BETWEEN OUR ROLES AS ADULTS, WITH ALL OF OUR POWER TO EVALUATE AND PUNISH, AND STUDENTS' OFTEN UNSPOKEN DESIRE TO BE SEEN AS WORTHY OF OUR ATTENTION.

A Curious Conversation lets a teacher and student do what cannot be done by the disciplinarians in the main office, guidance counselors, or other school support staff: build our own relationship with the student. For students who have rarely, if ever, felt safe and known in schools, a Curious Conversation can bridge the gap between our roles as adults, with all of our power to evaluate and punish, and students' often unspoken desire to be seen as worthy of our attention.

The goal of a Curious Conversation—for the student to connect with you—is more important than any single question you ask. The fact that you are asking the questions and listening to the answers precludes the need to ask the questions in a specific order. The way a student responds to one question will give you clues as to where your next inquiry can be most useful. For most students, the fact that you are honestly curious about them will, by itself, build bridges between the two of you. Follow your own curiosity as well—with each student, the path of the Curious Conversation is unique.

One rule is worth stating: Don't use the time to judge or try to teach the student a new skill. Hacking discipline is ultimately about the student repairing the harm done by their actions, regardless of their intentions—and students need to know that we want them to rebuild the relationship with us while we acknowledge the rule that was broken. Asking questions, listening, and responding with compassion are the building blocks of prevention.

We can use this classic phrase when we are listening in almost any situation: "Tell me more." These three simple words express your ongoing curiosity without guiding the speaker to a conclusion you may want to draw. If you're in a place in the conversation where you want to know more but aren't sure exactly how to phrase your curiosity, "Tell me more" is a universal option.

As adults in school, we sometimes forget to extend to students the same courtesies we would offer to people of our own age; in contrast, the Curiosity Conversation starts best when we ask the student if they are more comfortable with the door open, if they are comfortable enough in their chair, and if they want to tell us something first. Once you have established that you want the conversation to be a place for the student to feel safe and brave, you can say, "I hope when we are done talking, I will know more about how to help you be successful. But right now, I don't know you well enough to come up with plans. I am curious about who you are and how I can help you."

Questions for a Curious Conversation

Questions about teachers:

- Have you had a teacher who really worked well with you? Tell me about that—do you know what made that relationship work?
- Are there ways I teach that make it harder—or easier—for you to learn?

- Do you have any advice for me on how to be a good teacher for you?

Questions about the curriculum:

- Do you have a favorite subject(s)? Tell me more.
- Is there a subject that has always been hard for you? Is there any part of that subject that you remember understanding or liking?
- Do you read on your own for fun? If so, where and when do you read? Where do you get your books? Do you have a favorite book, genre, or author?
- (If the student is not an independent reader …) Have you ever finished reading a book? Tell me about that. Have you ever liked a book assigned in school, even if you didn't finish it? Did you fake that you read it just to get by? Do you read comics? If reading is hard, how long can you read before the words stop making sense: a page or two? Five minutes?
- Have you liked art or music or acting classes? Tell me more about them, please.

Questions about being a student:

- What's writing like for you? Tell me more. For instance, is it better by hand or keyboard? Do you know how to make an outline or other ways to prepare to write? Have you ever written something that *you* really liked? Tell me more.
- Is there a best place for you to sit to be a good student? Do you need a break now and then? Does it help if I

write directions on the board? Do you like working with others, would you rather work on your own, or does it depend on the task?

- Is there anything you can tell me about doing homework that helps you be successful?

Questions about their interests:

- What do you like to do for fun? (If the student says video games, be as curious as you would be if they said they played cello in an orchestra.) Which are your favorite games? What do you like about those games? How did you learn to play it? Do you think you are good at it? Do you think I would like it?

Questions to fix the harm done and prevent future harm:

- Do you have any ideas about how you can fix things up now? Let's brainstorm some ideas together.
- Would it help you if I set up a conversation with any of the other students to prevent future difficulties?
- When you are getting upset in school, what are some strategies you can use to avoid getting in trouble? Can we brainstorm a few ways I can help you use those strategies?

Questions to end the Curious Conversation:

- Do you want to tell me anything else?
- I learned this from our conversation: _________. Does that sound like I understood you?

Curious Conversations are wonderful to hold with all students, not just those who have misbehaved. Most teachers will prioritize their time by first attending to the students who are struggling—but a Curious Conversation with a typically on-task student has many benefits as well. However, those students aren't usually the ones who are now staying with you at lunch, during recess, and before and after school because they have misbehaved. Use that time to prevent instead of punish!

WHAT YOU CAN DO TOMORROW

FOR ADMINISTRATORS:

- **SHARE THE STRATEGIES OF CHILL-OUT PLANS AND CURIOUS CONVERSATIONS.** Offer these strategies to the staff without imposing any expectations. Compare these strategies to other school practices that are supported without being mandatory. If there is a Hacking Discipline Committee, members of that committee can volunteer to be early adopters. They can then share their experiences at staff meetings and via the school email lists. At this point, administrators are igniting interest and building capacity for more.
- **PREPARE TO BE PART OF A STUDENT'S CHILL-OUT PLAN.** When I was a principal, I was asked at times to help a student use their Chill-Out Plan when an adult was needed to monitor them outside the classroom. Some students asked if I could be a regular part of their plan–sadly, I had to say no to that

request because I couldn't be reliably available. Other students would escalate when "the principal" approached–I was not a good chill-out support for those students. When I was able to help out, I felt useful in ways I was rarely experiencing as one of the school's ultimate disciplinarians. I also gained the recognition and respect of the staff for getting down into the weeds with the work they do every day. Make sure the staff, including the main office administrative assistants, know you are eager to help out.

- **TRY A CURIOUS CONVERSATION.** In Hack 1, the school decided which misbehaviors would require administrative intervention with the students. In Hack 2, a Chill-Out Plan is listed as one of your strategies when developing a restorative plan and preparing misbehaving students to return to class. Take an upcoming opportunity to try a Curious Conversation when you can carve out the time and the student is not overtly resistant. Suggest that all the administrators who discipline students try a Curious Conversation. Then compare notes.

  Most often, the conversation happens when we are otherwise going to be talking to the student in a strictly disciplinary mode. Allocating time for punishment is already part of the school tradition–but punishment doesn't teach new behaviors or build new bonds. Turn the paradigm on its head and use the time to talk and listen! Both you and the student will gain much from what is often an exercise neither party finds satisfying.

FOR STAFF:

If you are a classroom teacher, you can develop Chill-Out Plans for your students. I have used such plans with students in elementary, middle, and high schools; adjust the language, array of choices, and autonomy permitted based on the developmental readiness of your students. Here are the important steps to get you going.

- **DECIDE WHERE TO BEGIN WITH CHILL-OUT PLANS.** You may want to set up Chill-Out Plans for all students right away to fast-track normalizing this into your classroom culture, or you may decide to start with a particular few who need it most. You will discover that certain students, particularly those with trauma histories, will most often implement their plans; they'll feel less in the spotlight knowing that others share the same need at some point.

  Share with students a starter list of chill-out options that are viable in your setting. Allow them to pick their three favorites. I have been surprised many times by what students already know works for them when they are given a list to choose from. A few students may need to experiment with you to discover what helps them chill out.

  You can offer options that are implemented outside the classroom if support staff are available to be with the student. Students in many schools are already receiving support services such as counseling; pull the support team into the planning.

- **DEVELOP AN UNOBTRUSIVE SIGNAL TO USE CHILL-OUT PLANS.** Many students do not want others to know they are in distress, further isolating them from seeking help. Students will appreciate an unobtrusive hand signal or a card they display to let you know when they want to use their plans. Staff can also develop their own discrete signals to use with students to silently suggest that the student use their plan at that time. A signal from an adult normalizes using plans, builds a relationship, and communicates to students that their need to chill out does not exclude them from the community of learning.
- **SHARE YOUR OWN CHILL-OUT PLANS WITH STUDENTS.** You do not have to share anything too personal, the background of your choices, or all your strategies. You are helping them normalize having strong feelings and serving as a role model for managing those feelings–all in the interest of helping the school day go well. Choose your chill-out strategies to share that are the simplest for them to understand and may serve as a springboard to their decision-making process. I typically told my students, "I know that when I am upset, I like to pace back and forth and grumble a little. Walking helps me chill out so I can hear myself think better. What can help you?"

A BLUEPRINT FOR FULL IMPLEMENTATION

For Administrators:

STEP 1: Consider a schoolwide implementation of Chill-Out Plans.

- **Provide training on implementation strategies:** In various settings, provide a forum for teachers who have piloted Chill-Out Plans to share their classroom implementation stories. For other staff members who are supporting students in using their plans, provide a script, such as: "I am here to help you with your Chill-Out Plan. What plan are you using now?" The staff person is not expected to provide counseling, lectures, or advice, and in many cases, does not need a preexisting close relationship with the student.
- **Build an array of approved and supported chill-out strategies:** At a staff meeting, provide time for brainstorming. Hacking Discipline Committee members can talk with their peers to further add to the array. A database can house the accumulating list of strategies, and the list can be supplemented by identifying the resources, such as fidgeting items, that the school approves for purchase.
- **Communicate with the community:** Many families may already know how their children chill out and can serve as a resource for the school's array of strategies. Other families may learn from the school how to help their children chill out; the synergy between home and school can be a powerful teaching moment for all.
- **Identify when the school is ready for a mandate:** When those implementing Chill-Out Plans have shown

enough practice and evidence of success, the school may reach a tipping point when it's ready for all students to have Chill-Out Plans. In Hack 5, we discussed that the administration does not need 100 percent of staff to accept a mandate, as is the case here. Administrators build capacity, provide support, gather stories and data, and use their influence, political capital, and ultimate authority to require needed change.

STEP 2: Document outcomes of Curious Conversations.

For schools that have a functioning Child Study Team (often mandated structures that consider what services the school can offer to struggling students), that team can include Curious Conversations in its checklist of interventions. The team can provide summary forms for the staff members who conduct the conversations, and track changes in the students' performance at their subsequent meetings.

For Staff:

STEP 1: Share Chill-Out Plans with families.

In the absence of a schoolwide effort to share the Chill-Out Plans, explain to families how the plans are working in your classroom. I have had many students who appreciated the adults in their homes learning this strategy. You can do this through an email and can go more in-depth with those who attend Family Night, when the adults from home have scheduled meetings with their children's teachers.

STEP 2: Develop a chill-out zone.

Most of the classrooms that work with our youngest students have a "quiet corner" where students can curl up on a beanbag chair, stare out the window, or look at a book. This practice should be continued for older students and adapted to age-appropriate needs and resources. The option to have a Chill-Out Plan that allows students to leave their chairs without having to leave the room is significant for helping students de-escalate and quickly return to the lesson. Sometimes, they only need a couple of minutes away from the group. Similar to having unobtrusive signals between students and teachers to use a Chill-Out Plan, the signals can include using the chill-out zone.

STEP 3: Conduct Curious Conversations throughout the year.

A Curious Conversation can happen without a precipitating event of misbehavior or a crisis. Depending on the staffing in a school, teachers can set aside fifteen minutes from a prep period (often requiring a bit of negotiating with another staff member) to have a conversation with a student. In some schools, there is an opportunity to have lunch with a student while conducting the conversation. The time spent upfront getting to know a student will be gained back many times by building a trusting relationship through listening in order to better know and plan for how this student functions.

These steps and the plan for full implementation correspond with the April–May sample schedule in Hack 1.

OVERCOMING PUSHBACK

All educators use tools to reduce the likelihood of student misbehavior. Engaging a school community in sharing those tools—moving from implicit to explicit practices—can build unity and creativity. Adding additional resources and strategies to toolkits does not immediately require universal changes. As staff integrate and share their new practices, their peers will become increasingly accepting of adding those tools to their current collection.

Students will ask to chill out to avoid academic challenges. Before I used Chill-Out Plans, many of my challenging students were spacing out excessively, randomly, and silently in their seats, with no support and no time limits, often until they misbehaved. I much prefer that they communicate, even if they do so too often at first. If students are keeping up with the lessons, despite what I might think is excessive chilling out, then I would do nothing to change their plans. If a student begins to demonstrate problems from their Chill-Out Plan, then it is time to change their plan, with the benefit that you are changing a plan, not trying to change a student. Most students, most of the time, will use the plan as it is designed to be used—and predictably, a few won't. Denying all students the right to a plan because a few peers will misuse their plans is detrimental to the greater good.

This feels infantilizing for high school students. Try this three-minute activity: Ask your students to share with the class, if they are comfortable doing so, how they chill out. You might model sharing first. Through their responses, your students will let you know whether they found the question infantilizing—I am guessing, from years of experience, that the answer will be that it is not infantilizing at all. Managing their emotional and cognitive changes is a foundational developmental task most teenagers are working through. The fact that they have not already been asked this question is the problem, not that the question might be infantilizing.

I don't want to share my own chill-out strategies. You don't have to. Teachers need to set boundaries on what they are comfortable sharing. You might substitute your current strategies with ones you used when you were young. Whether you actually loved to draw when you were young is not the point—only that you keep the student on task. The focus is always to support the work of the student.

Curious Conversations sound too much like therapy. It's a good thing when teachers are worried about stepping into the role of therapist, and it suggests that we need to define the boundary between therapy and Curious Conversations. The conversation does not ask anything about a student's home life or intimate personal history. If concerns are emerging in those areas, the teacher can let the student know how to access the support services in the school.

The goal of the conversation is for the adult to gain insights into structuring the student's *school* day for success. The questions are about how the students have managed the demands of school and what they know about themselves as learners. The secondary benefit of building a better adult-student relationship will invariably support more success in school—all through a compassionate and endless curiosity in how this student functions as a learner.

THE HACK IN ACTION

Mr. P, the physical education teacher, stuck his head into the principal's office. "Anna, do you have a few minutes to talk?"

"Yes, this is a good time," she said. She closed her computer, got up from behind her desk, and motioned for Mr. P to join her in a small sitting area by her window.

He reached back, shut the office door, and sat down. "I don't mean to be a problem with this Chill-Out Plan idea. I mean, I like the ideas a lot. You know I've been enthusiastic about the Hacking Discipline Committee—although I think changing the name to "The Teaching Better Behaviors Committee" is a bit much—but otherwise, I am all on board. I've been piloting each hack we've done along the way and talking it up in the teachers' lounge and at meetings. Some staff have started to look to me for ideas and support to try out new strategies … so I wanted to let you know all that because I don't think I can do the Chill-Out Plans, and I don't want you to think I'm being a problem or something like that."

"Mr. P," Anna said, "you've been a wonderful addition to the staff. And I haven't said that everyone has to do the Chill-Out Plans, so please don't worry if you can't do them. We are still piloting this. It's okay."

"Thank you," Mr. P said, sighing in relief. "But I wanted to also tell you that my difficulty with the Chill-Out Plans might be a structural problem we have to address. I kind of heard this from some of the other specialist teachers; I'd rather not say who."

"That's okay," Anna said. "Structural problems aren't the fault of a single staff person, nor can a single person solve them. And I am not going to shoot the messenger when there is a structural problem I need to know about. So, I don't care who else spoke to you about this. Tell me the problem."

He took a deep breath and said quickly, "I just have too many students to do this with each one or to remember what they have in their plans, or to have all the fidgety stuff and headphones that classroom teachers have. I see half the students in the school. It's just too much."

They sat quietly for a moment.

"But I do have an idea," Mr. P said, his voice regaining its typical enthusiasm. "What if I identify four or five chill-out options to do in the gym or the field, ones that I think most kids could use? Then, if there's a student who really needs something different, I'll work with their teacher or counselor to pick out one for them to use in my class. Yeah, that would work. Then I would only have to remember a small number of individualized plans—I have to do that with kids on IEPs anyway—while everyone else sticks to the four or five chill-out strategies that are for use with me. I could do that."

"Mr. P, I think that would work. And it serves the goal of this hack: making sure students and their teachers are on the same page about chilling out."

"Great," Mr. P said. "And we could bring this to the committee first, but I could talk to the other specialist teachers about my plan and tell them they can try it in their classes."

"I love it," said Anna. "Go ahead and do that. We can share your story with the committee, but let's not wait until then to get you started. We are still very much in our test run phases. Your test run will give us even more data about integrating Chill-Out Plans into the school culture."

"All right, I'm on it," Mr. P said, popping up from his chair. "Thank you so much for your time. This will be interesting ..." His voice trailed off as he closed the door and then quickly reopened it, stuck his head into Anna's office again, and said, "But those Curious Conversations! Boy, am I going to have a lot of fun with them."

"I am sure you will," Anna replied.

The most obvious benefit to Chill-Out Plans and Curious Conversations will be that students better manage the feelings that lead to misbehaviors. For a good number of students, this self-knowledge and the connected strategies will improve their chances of success wherever they go. For a handful, this may save their lives.

For the staff, focusing on prevention versus intervention means they will less often have to implement their own chill-out strategies to get through the day because students will be using their strategies first.

For Administrators:

- What barriers would interfere with your piloting Curious Conversations in your work with misbehaving students, and how do you remove those barriers?
- How can you schedule support staff to be available to help a student with an outside-the-classroom chill-out strategy?

- Which chill-out strategies would you like to see become uniformly part of your school culture?

For Staff:

- How do you chill out at school?
- In what ways does the culture of your school already support the need for students to chill out, and how have you accommodated that culture in your work?
- Looking at the questions for Curious Conversations, which ones seem most interesting for use with your students?

HACK 9

COMPILE AND COMMUNICATE

CREATE THE NECESSARY TECH INFRASTRUCTURE

Data is not information, information is not knowledge, knowledge is not understanding, understanding is not wisdom.

— CLIFFORD STOLL, ASTRONOMER, TEACHER, AUTHOR

THE PROBLEM: THERE IS NO CONSISTENT DATA TO INFORM DISCIPLINE DECISIONS

EVERY DAY IN a school, innumerable adult-student experiences are associated with discipline. Even in a school with a strong disciplinarian, that person needs a system to track all those experiences, to analyze the strengths and weaknesses of the system, and to suggest needed changes. If all that responsibility is kept with one person, the school reduces the possibilities of systemic improvement, leading to misunderstandings, the duplication of efforts, and an inefficient use of resources.

An inadequate tracking system prevents schools from addressing many root problems of discipline. In middle schools and high schools, a single student can have as many as eight teachers in a single day. In all grades, a student will cross paths with many adults: administrators, administrative assistants, nurses, librarians, aides, and lunchroom monitors. However, the lunchroom monitors and the librarian may have no means to share and compare their efforts—the student is the only one who holds the experience of all those encounters.

Every interaction a student has with an adult can impact their next adult encounter. A student who does wonderfully in physical education may struggle in an art class, whether it's because of their relationship with the teacher, their previous experiences with learning art, or the person sitting next to the student in that class. And the reverse may be true for the student sitting one row back. Keeping track of who struggles throughout the day is one of the hardest and most important tasks for any teacher or administrator.

FROM A DISCIPLINE PERSPECTIVE, TECHNOLOGY AND DATA ARE FOUNDATION BLOCKS THAT SUPPORT US IN HELPING ALL THE STUDENTS IN OUR SCHOOLS.

The adults in schools also react to students through the lens of their own backgrounds. We all have preexisting biases. A student who gets along well with one teacher may not behave the same way with a different teacher, perhaps resulting from their cultural and generational upbringings, with all the expectations and morals that make us who we are. These differences and biases are part of a school community. The absence of a tracking system can leave the system unable to hack the biases impacting school discipline. School staff often have conflicting relationships with technology. In some schools, the administration fully embraces technology, while teachers feel wary that it will negatively impact their jobs. In other schools, the administrators are worried about an overuse of technology, whereas the teachers are begging for more tools in their toolboxes. The word "technology," in some settings, has become a pejorative. All these problems combine to form one of the largest challenges of any discipline system: keeping track of all those adult-student disciplinary experiences.

From a discipline perspective, technology and data are foundation blocks that support us in helping all the students in our schools—but they come with many hurdles to clear. It's time to hack the technology and data that improve discipline outcomes.

THE HACK: COMPILE AND COMMUNICATE

The infrastructure for tracking discipline experiences—the hardware, applications, formatting options, and ease of use—need to fit into the school's technology culture with minimal disruption in order to facilitate staff compliance. In most school systems and in the larger school community, IT resources can build a tracking system to manage your needs. If your school has already installed and implemented a robust student information system (SIS), adding additional features to track discipline events will not present a big challenge to the existing technology culture.

On the school culture level—especially how staff talk with each other about students—the tracking of discipline events can have a significant impact. The behavioral incidents we choose to track or ignore, and the conversations we hold to understand those incidents, present opportunities for both enlightenment and conflict. What had most often been private experiences between students and adults will now become accessible for others to analyze.

One of the best practices to forestall conflict and instead build a more coherent school culture is to share a common language and construct for analyzing the behaviors we track. When a school community embraces the following sequence, and the school leaders reliably lead conversations that follow this sequence, then you are more likely to foster the school culture you want. The sequence is: Data, Information, Knowledge, and Wisdom.

Data—Data is simply the raw numbers. For example, twelve students were late to class after lunch on Tuesday, two students were fighting at recess this week, and eight students violated the technology usage rules this month. *Data does not demand any particular course of action*—that may be the most important notion from this sequence. Jumping from data to actions invites overreach, exclusion of diverse perspectives, and unintended consequences. The more staff members who understand that data does not demand a particular course of action, the less likely the system will be to make that error. In other words, just because twelve students were late to class after lunch on Tuesday does not mean we must add additional staff to lunch duty. A school culture that fosters immediate actions based on the most recent data needs a strong understanding of this sequence. Data does not explain; data needs to be explained.

Information—In this step, we begin to organize the data into trends and patterns. Be aware of the choices being made to use averages, percentages, and multiple increases or decreases—those choices can unduly influence further analysis. For instance, "There was a 50 percent decrease in behavioral incidents in the lunchroom this week" doesn't tell us exactly how many more incidents occurred. Keep the original data available for deeper reflection as you take the next step. Leaders can build and extend a professional culture of seeking multiple perspectives as they turn data into information.

Knowledge—When we look at the information we created and apply it to our mission and goals, we construct knowledge. We ask each other, "Do we have a problem?" We examine the varied forces that are at play in our system and begin to wonder about the root causes of persistent issues that emerged from collecting data. This question—"Do we have a problem?"—helps position the school for calm reflection concerning groups of students, structural weaknesses in schedules, and the flow of communication between administration and staff.

Wisdom—If a problem has been identified in the knowledge step, we can now consider if, how, and when to address the problem. We apply our collective wisdom. We research how other schools handled this problem and identify the resources to leverage or add. We are strategic in hacking discipline.

THE PATTERNS OF MISBEHAVIORS FOR A GIVEN STUDENT OR A COHORT OF STUDENTS CAN INFORM A SCHOOL'S APPROACH TO PREVENTION, THE IDENTIFICATION OF EFFECTIVE ADULT RESPONSES, AND SUCCESSFUL REENTRY PLANS.

The sequence can take place within a single meeting or over a period of days. Sharing this sequence with staff can support their examination of test scores and their own behavioral data. Sharing and implementing this sequence can soothe anxieties that unexplained data will lead to impulsive actions. The Hacking Discipline Committee can follow and model this sequence, supporting a culture that can more easily embrace data collection, knowing how that data will be analyzed for the greater good.

WHAT YOU CAN DO TOMORROW

FOR ADMINISTRATORS (PRIMARILY):

The tasks in this section are largely in the purview of administrators, who have the authority and resources to implement schoolwide technology systems. A Hacking Discipline Committee can be a sounding board for giving administrators feedback regarding their choices and assessing the readiness of the staff to do their part.

- **DECIDE WHAT STUDENT INFORMATION YOU NEED.** Discipline incidents are about real students who come to school with an array of personal characteristics and backgrounds. Hack 4 examined the structural elements of schools that influence misbehaviors; by addressing those elements, schools can reduce misbehaviors. Similarly, the *patterns* of misbehaviors for a given student or a cohort of students can inform a school's approach to prevention, the identification of effective adult responses, and successful reentry plans. Data can reveal those patterns.

  Those patterns may also reveal long-held assumptions and expectations about particular cohorts of students. For instance, the origin of the word "dumb," meaning of limited intelligence, was based on a historical misunderstanding about people who were mute; they were considered less intelligent. Now we know there is no correlation between people who are mute and their intelligence, character, or potential. We collect data about our current cohorts of students to ensure they are not similarly misunderstood, and therefore more vulnerable, because of their demographic identities. If an outsized number of a student minority is being disciplined in the school, looking at the data can help a school recognize biases and then do the difficult work of constructing information, knowledge, and wisdom.

  Many large school systems already require tracking students by their cohorts. A given school may choose to include additional data. Here is a typical demographic data set for students:

- race
- ethnicity
- gender identity
- religion
- special education status
- 504 plan status
- English language learner (ELL)
- FARMS status
- grade level/year of graduation
- birthdate (could tell you whether the student is "young" or "old" for their grade)
- assessment scores
- anything else you can think of

When identifying data your staff needs, it is better to have too much rather than too little. You don't have to use all the data that gets input, but if you don't record it, you won't be able to use it in the future.

- **DECIDE WHAT INCIDENT INFORMATION YOU NEED.** A discipline incident involving students and adults can be looked at through the widest lenses to capture the relevant data related to the incident–and "relevant" needs to be defined by every school that develops a hacking discipline system. This second set of data could include:

- student name
- behavior reporter's name
- behavior
- witness(es)
- location of behavior
- desired plan of action
- administrative response
- long-term plans

- **ASSESS ADMINISTRATION READINESS TO USE TRACKING APPLICATIONS.** The entire staff will need to be familiar with data entry, using whatever application is chosen. The administration has a greater task: knowing how to organize the data into the initial draft of useful information. Administrators need familiarity with the application. Even if a "techie" in the school will create the actual form and merge the actual data, it is extremely useful for the administrators to know how to use the spreadsheet software. If terms like "pivot table," "lookup," and "conditional formatting" sound like nonsense to administrators, they need to learn the software.

A BLUEPRINT FOR FULL IMPLEMENTATION

STEP 1: Make data entry quick and easy.

A form is an easy way to get information about behavioral incidents from the staff to the administration. No matter what software your school uses, online forms should be quickly and easily accessible by all the key stakeholders. In addition, the forms need to feed the data into a spreadsheet. This, while it sounds simplistic, is incredibly important to implementation. An administrator or tech integrationist at your school should have no problem exporting the form data to a spreadsheet that can then allow the data to be analyzed.

The best people to give feedback regarding the convenience of a form are the end-users. Disseminate drafts of the form to staff—or to the Hacking Discipline Committee, get feedback, and revise.

STEP 2: Train staff how and when to use the form.

If you want all staff members to have access to the form to submit information about behavior incidents, it needs to be in a quick and convenient place for everyone to access. If the school has an intranet, internal website, or even a heavily used quick-links document, the form should be linked there. Listen to the staff to find out the best location for the form. Provide training for new staff and offer a "cheat sheet" of all the basic input processes, including a model of the input form filled out correctly.

STEP 3: Pull the data together.

Merging the data is the next key piece to the program. If you can't reliably merge your data, moving from data to information is nearly impossible. Most SIS programs have a truly dizzying amount of data stored inside. The school administrator or tech integrationist should know how to pull out the necessary data if they know what to look for. Again, knowing what you want to collect is the first step in any data infrastructure.

STEP 4: Decide who can see the data.

The collection of data increases anxiety. Be clear about who will have access to the inputted data each day. Every administrator? One particular administrator who is collecting all the data? There are often concerns about confidentiality when it comes to accessing information, so spend time discussing who should have that access. The tech person who is creating the input form and spreadsheet is probably not the person who should access the data unless their job function demands it. The person who creates the form transfers ownership to whoever needs access.

STEP 5: Develop a shared data-to-wisdom culture.

Many schools already have grade-level teams and department teams examining test scores. Administrators can sit in on those meetings to model the data-to-wisdom process for what is already part of the school culture. Administrators can also provide simple summary worksheets that identify each step of the process, and they can ask for those worksheets to be shared with them. The same approach can be taken with Child Study Teams. An ongoing Hacking Discipline Committee will be an ideal forum for developing a sustained culture of moving from data to wisdom as administrators ponder the meaning of the data in their system.

These steps and the plan for full implementation correspond with the May–June sample schedule in Hack 1.

OVERCOMING PUSHBACK

It is said that children who grow up using the latest technology are like native speakers of a language; everyone else is a technology immigrant. Staff pushback should not be seen simply as a resistance to change when schools move to greater use of technology and data. Much pushback can be averted when staff know their concerns are being validated. Administrators can discuss their pathways to learning the tracking system and listen to the challenges others are experiencing—the staff will then be more likely to invest in being part of the solution.

This is confidential data! We can't have it online. People may be concerned with putting data online. We've all heard stories of companies and government agencies getting hacked and having their data compromised. Data that is completely unconnected to the internet is safer from some form of intrusion. Acknowledging such concerns and discussing your safety plans are better than ignoring those concerns.

The IT director in a school can share with staff the many safeguards built into every system. If the school is using a standard cloud-based system, such as Google or Microsoft 365, your data is password-protected, along with several other system-level security features. In most schools, the data is significantly difficult to access without authorized clearance.

Assuring confidentiality is why the technology chapter is not at the beginning of the book; the IT staff can develop the data tracking system while all the other steps of hacking discipline, fielding concerns and adjusting formats, are in process. As in all the other Hacks, transparency in the process offers the best method to thoroughly vet the system and simultaneously build staff buy-in.

Ultimately, all schools must store data somewhere. It is likely that your school's internet security is exponentially safer than a filing cabinet in the main office.

This data will be used to punish teachers for disciplining students. When staff members need to be spoken to about concerns in the data, the conversations should follow the protocols outlined in collective bargaining agreements that already exist. Data in the tracking system has as much or as little weight as the classroom observations and the other evaluation components that school leaders use in conversations and decision-making regarding staff. The construct of moving from data to information to knowledge to wisdom, discussed earlier in this chapter, applies as much to staff as it does to students. Data alone does not explain anything; it is the data that needs explaining. The administration can also address this concern by plainly stating that this data will not be used in staff evaluations during a test run period that may need to last one to three years. In certain school districts, this language can be built into collective bargaining agreements.

Staff members won't consistently input data. Again, this is why the conversations with staff, whether through a Hacking Discipline Committee or other means of communication, need to happen before a tracking system is online. Test runs through the development process will help identify any glitches in teacher compliance. Through the test runs and the launching of the tracking system, administrators must prioritize responding consistently to the data input initiated by staff. When staff members see the administration and their peers taking the process seriously, they are more likely to buy into the process themselves. Ultimately, inputting data is a job-performance expectation equivalent to tracking attendance and grades. The administration can demarcate a grace period when the tracking system is launched and offer coaching for those who may find it daunting to get started.

None of the administrators are skilled enough to create this system. Creating the tracking system does require a specific skill set. Other schools in the area, or schools found through an internet search, may be willing to share their basic tools. There's also a good chance that someone on the staff is well-versed in online forms and spreadsheets. With cloud-based tracking systems, one person can create the basic forms and then transfer ownership to an administrator so the creator of the system doesn't maintain access to the system once it is launched. The more important role of administration is to maintain needed transparency in the process.

I've been doing this work for years now and have never needed this kind of technological infrastructure to manage behavior. Comfort with a traditional practice does not mean that the practice has served staff and students well enough. Technology systems can identify trends, duplication of efforts, missed opportunities to improve student outcomes, and inequities that have been hidden in plain sight for too long. Discipline tracking systems, accessible to staff and administration versus one administrator, allow safeguards against possible mismanagement or biases. A technological infrastructure that makes data easier to analyze and supports all parties having a measure of responsibility can improve everyone's quality of life.

THE HACK IN ACTION

"Show of hands," said Anna, opening the Hacking Discipline Committee meeting to approve the online tracking form. "How many of you consider yourselves computer geeks? Let me say first, I am definitely not raising my hand, and I am jealous of anyone who raises their hand."

A small number of the committee members put their hands up.

"I am going to assume that you are representative of the entire faculty," Anna said. "We won't have the staff hugging us for adding to their time on computers."

Maria, the assistant principal, jumped in. "But they'll see that the time spent putting their misbehavior incidents into the system will ultimately save us all a lot of time. And you can do the entry really fast!" She paused. "Did I just jump too far ahead?"

"Well, yes," Anna said, "but you demonstrate a split on the staff that is happening in schools all over the country: some people are eager to jump into technology, and some people are wary, and nobody is wrong to be who they are."

Ms. S, the English department chair, spoke up. "Let me share my experience with this. When we do the data dives each quarter, scanning through the reading test scores, my eyes blur over. I simply can't do it. But my department has been piloting the data-to-wisdom process for the last couple of years. They know how overwhelmed I feel at the data stage—but I am really excited by the conversations at the information, knowledge, and wisdom stages. That's when I jump in. The department changed the sequence of novels we read in each grade through that discussion last spring. I don't think we need everyone to be a data geek to benefit from having data."

"As for me," Mr. P, the physical education teacher, said, "just tell me what to do. Give me the headlines—I think that's the wisdom stage—and I can make it work with my students. I don't need to know anything else."

"I love the data dive!" Ms. R, the guidance director, said. "I love the give-and-take, the kicking around of theories, and the deciding on a course of action. Those conversations, when we go from the data to the wisdom all together, get everyone on board and committed to the work ahead."

"Let me stop you all here," Anna said. "You have jumped ahead of today's agenda—although you have definitely made me even more cognizant of the task of this committee, and my task as a principal to assure the staff that we will introduce the technology expectations in a clear way. The departments who piloted the data-to-wisdom process have told me many times how useful that process has been. We'll need to apply it to our behavioral data when we have that data. My current thinking is that a subset of this group will continue doing the initial work of taking us from data to information on behaviors. I don't want any one person—not me, not

Maria, not any one person—doing the data-to-information step on their own. We have to check each other's biases and perspectives."

She continued, "But today, we are going to look at the first iteration of the form for inputting behavior incidents into the tracking systems. Open your computers. We'll all try it. We need to hear if it is easy to use, if the categories are correct, and if anything could be improved. Once we gather our ideas, we will ask another set of teachers to pilot it and give us more feedback. By the next time we meet, we should have a tracking system ready to launch—but only when we have done the training. Then we'll do one larger test run."

"We have to get this right," Anna concluded. "Hacking discipline will only be as good as the quality of the day-to-day experiences that are in the tracking system, which will only be as good as the training and support we give to staff."

"Data" and "technology" have become pejoratives among many educators as we face unknown societal upheaval wrought by computers, the internet, artificial intelligence, and social media. Understandably, any further investment in technology can trigger significant concerns. We are all coping in various ways with the impacts of living through a technological revolution.

For Administrators:

- What supports do you need to lead the technology and data part of hacking discipline?
- In what ways might you encounter resistance to categorizing students by race, gender identity, etc., in the tracking system?

- What opportunities are currently in your school to pilot the data-to-wisdom process?

For Staff:

- How can you effectively share your recommendations and concerns with those building the technology for the hacking discipline system data?
- What opportunities do you have in your role to use the data-to-wisdom process?
- What safeguards are in the staff evaluation process in your school so that data entry on discipline will be used equitably by evaluators?

HACK 10

BUILD THE FUTURE NOW

LEVERAGE RESOURCES TO MAINTAIN THE MOMENTUM

You never change things by fighting the existing reality. To change something, build a new model that makes the existing model obsolete.

— R. Buckminster Fuller, architect and philosopher

THE PROBLEM: IMPLEMENTATION REQUIRES CONTINUED EFFORT

The complexity, pressure, and insufficient resources granted to schools present enormous barriers to sustained growth and change. Even as the administration or hacking committee shared drafts, sought input, experimented with test runs, and explored needed structural changes—hopefully creating a positive buzz for a better future—the old ways of discipline had another year of wrapping themselves around the school culture. Presenting the schoolwide plan to hack discipline, explored in Hack 7, is closer to the beginning of success than it is to the end, when the structures and routines fully manifest a culture of calm and restorative responses to student misbehavior.

One common barrier: Every year, schools introduce new innovations. Veteran teachers will have seen the introductions of many innovations. Not all of these have become part of their work. Funding to sustain training and resources can disappear. Changes in administration often upend the school's priorities. The demands of a standardized curriculum and the hyper-focus on academic test scores present barriers to new initiatives. The innovation may have been presented as a "best practice" but can have glitches that undermine a commitment to the process. Schools have an incalculable burden or comfort in how discipline has always been handled in schools, and no guarantee that the innovation will reap benefits worth the effort to use it. Finally, teachers have classes filled with marvelously idiosyncratic and diverse students who deter a lot of the adult plans. Integrating discipline changes into the complex history and dynamics of schools has proven to be a challenge.

I have never heard a school system proclaim to all its stakeholders and staff, "This year, we are completing the work on hacking discipline and doing nothing else new! One new initiative, that's all! We are focusing on reaching greater competency and mastery based on one plan. If we can do that, the school will be more successful with more students compared to anything else we can do."

Unfortunately, there is no guarantee that mastering what is already expected of schools will expand the limitations that are wired into the structural DNA of our educational system. Schools operate in an imperfect world, one that has never found the commitment and resources to do much more than replicate the dysfunction and inequities of the status quo. So much can be improved! The status quo is not an ideal worth fighting for; neither is an endless parade of the latest innovations that are diminished by the next shiny innovation. Being busy is not the same as being strategic in the long run. So many promising initiatives become marginalized.

Another year without hacking discipline means another cohort of students will become accustomed to the culture of punishment. The same will be true for the newest staff members, often at the beginning of their careers. As children, most of them attended schools with traditional approaches to discipline. As they experience that approach through orientation, the stories of their peers, and their experiences now as teachers with misbehaving students, they, too, can become a barrier to change.

Equally problematic is that they will likely hear about any history of unfulfilled innovations. They will have questions about the hacking discipline plan and the work done to create that plan—but without follow-through to root that plan into the culture of the school, the newest staff begin to develop a layer of cynicism that will resonate with the veteran staff. All initiatives will be suspect.

The problems of misbehavior and traditional discipline impact every adult and every student every day in every setting, and some students far more than others. Hacking discipline requires everyone to follow through, over and around the barriers. The hard work continues into a second year for those committed to making a difference.

THE HACK: BUILD THE FUTURE NOW

An excellent tool for identifying and leveraging the resources to finish the hacking discipline initiative is articulated in the management book *Reframing Organizations* by Lee Bolman and Terrence Deal. The authors urge leaders to operate in four frames: structural, human resource, political, and symbolic. By applying actions in all four frames, the synergy among those actions communicates alignment across the board.

Inspired by those four frames, a Hacking Discipline Committee or administrative team can create a custom framework to communicate to the school community, "This is how we use student misbehaviors to build skills, accountability, and relationships. This is how we roll around here."

Following are four similar frames to use in an education setting: Procedures, Supports, Diplomacy, and Culture. Many of the actions can fit into multiple frames—suggesting that the actions will have a greater impact. For instance, "Scheduling team and department time to share stories and problem-solve" is listed in the Supports frame because of its power to help staff develop skills and confidence. That action can also be in the Procedures frame as it fits into an organized schedule. Such meetings impact the Culture because they communicate to everyone that the hacking discipline initiative remains of primary importance.

Procedures—In this frame, schools are seen as large machines with parts needing to be in place and well maintained. Administrators use their authority for hacking discipline to define, clarify, communicate, and uphold standard operating procedures. For instance, they provide clearly written protocols and checklists that all staff can access in the school's online documents, including:

- misbehaviors that require administrative responses
- misbehaviors that belong to the staff
- menu of responses to student misbehaviors
- checklist for returning a student to class
- list of chill-out options
- questions for a prevention conversation
- instructions for entering data into the student information system

Supports—In this frame, schools are seen as communities of people who need and support each other—a place. Our adult connections and affiliations are essential for staff to collectively buy into the restorative discipline practices, including:

- Schedule team, grade-level, and department time to share stories and problem-solve.
- Provide peer coaches and mentors.
- Develop new staff orientation on restorative practices.
- Offer readings and videos.
- Invite staff from other schools who have restorative discipline practices.

Diplomacy—This frame identifies strategic actions that bring influential people, groups, and forces to support the hacking discipline initiative. At times, that strategic action also means protecting the initiative from interference, such as bureaucratic red tape, until the plan is ready to launch. The Diplomacy frame can include:

- adding a key member or two to the Hacking Discipline Committee
- keeping superintendents and school boards informed
- seeking coverage in local news media
- holding question-and-answer sessions with parent organizations

Culture—This frame reinforces a shared culture that will influence all the restorative discipline decisions (i.e., this is how we respond to student misbehavior). School leaders are *always* working in the Culture frame, explicitly and implicitly supporting restorative practices. Teachers play the same role in their classrooms. While items in all the other frames carry weight through their inclusion in the community, the following are additional actions that impact Culture:

- Provide time for invested staff to share stories in the community.
- Offer funding for additional reading and research.
- Support in-school observations and visits to other schools.
- Publish updates and data in newsletters.
- Display posters in hallways about restorative practices and forgiveness.
- Share stories from students who earned back trust and privileges.

School cultures and histories are like the tides in the ocean—powerful enough to throw a large ship off course. The four frames are a reminder that hacking discipline is much more than any single decision, checklist, or presentation. A school needs a powerful engine and many hands on deck to maintain momentum in the right direction.

WHAT YOU CAN DO TOMORROW

FOR ADMINISTRATORS OR THE HACKING DISCIPLINE COMMITTEE:

- **DECIDE THE SIZE OF YOUR LAUNCH.** Even with all the test runs and feedback up to this point, there is a big difference between working with a motivated group of early adopters versus an entire school staff. If you feel you have done the preliminary hacks sufficiently, a full-scale launch makes a clear statement: "This is now who we are." Clear your agenda as much as possible during the first few days in order to be available for problem-solving small glitches; coordinate schedules with other school leaders so that one of you is always available. Be most ready to do the part of the job that belongs to the main office: working with the students sent to you for misbehavior and working the plans to get them back to class.

A soft launch is also possible. Perhaps a grade-level or a middle school team can take the system through one more test run for a day or two. A soft launch gives more assurance that all parts of the plan are functioning before the entire school is involved. Let the rest of the staff know the length of the soft launch and the predicted day for all to implement the new system.

- **REINFORCE NONNEGOTIABLES FOR THE INITIAL DAYS OF THE LAUNCH.** Remember that all the staff will not remember equally well the same aspects of the hacking discipline plan; each will have a learning curve until it is second nature. Establish the initial priorities. Support the staff and help build coherence by underscoring a small number of nonnegotiables from day one.
- **CHOOSE IMPLEMENTATION DATA POINTS.** Early on, such as the first week of the launch, look for data that underscores staff buy-in and administrator follow-through. It is too soon to know the impact on student behavior, relationships, and accountability—all

of that will be the result of staff implementation of the plan.

- **SHARE THE WISDOM.** Disseminate the early data—and the pathway from that data to the information, knowledge, and wisdom that will inform any adjustments. And remember to celebrate the small steps of success! Doing so boosts the Culture (sharing the successes raises their importance). It's also in the Supports frame (underscoring the teamwork and affiliation needed to hack discipline) and potentially the Diplomacy frame (highlighting the successes that build your coalition).

A BLUEPRINT FOR FULL IMPLEMENTATION

STEP 1: Review the checklist for hacking an entire school's discipline system.

All the prior Hacks in this book have prepared the school for the full implementation of a hacking discipline plan. The well-known Lippitt-Knoster matrix of six critical factors guiding complex change in an organization can be your checklist to assess where more preparation can lead to a better launch. You don't need to have everything perfectly aligned; the checklist can warn you where you might anticipate implementation dips. See Image 10.1 for an example checklist to hack an entire school's discipline system.

CHECKLIST OF SIX CRITICAL FACTORS IN HACKING AN ENTIRE SCHOOL'S DISCIPLINE SYSTEM

	What we have done so far	What else we can do
Have we communicated the vision of a better discipline system?		
Do we have enough staff buy-in, approaching consensus, to launch?		
Have we given staff enough practice to build their skills in using the data system and in responding to misbehaviors?		
What incentives do we offer for staff to invest their time and effort in the new system?		
Are the resources in place for supporting the staff, and do the staff know how to access them?		
Is our action plan clear and available?		

Image 10.1

STEP 2: Craft a yearlong timeline.

A timeline is a version of your action plan that includes the critical opportunities for staff to provide feedback. Hack 1 recommended crafting a timeline that included writing and distributing drafts of protocols, brainstorming strategies, collecting feedback on those strategies, testing procedures, and presenting a plan. The next timeline will focus on fully implementing all the components of the plan. This timeline will also help soothe staff concerns that they are expected to be fully competent from the first day. Staff need to know that there will be someone in charge of correcting implementation glitches.

Here is a sample of what this second timeline can include:

June–August

- Enter forms and lists into the school's information system.
- Develop staff orientation to the new discipline system.
- Summarize known information on student misbehaviors to track changes.
- Set initial goals for the plan implementation.

September–October

- Orient staff to the new system.
- Provide outreach to parents.
- Ensure all administrators and staff are inputting behavioral incidents via the new forms.

- Move from data to wisdom on staff implementation successes and struggles.
- Do a first quarter comparison of former misbehavior information to current data.
- Develop protocols for staff seeking peer coaching and feedback.
- Adjust and set new goals for the plan implementation.
- Celebrate successes.

November–December

- Survey the new system.
- Provide administrative feedback on using a variety of responses to student misbehaviors.
- Collect staff feedback on using a variety of responses to student misbehaviors.
- Assess the frequency of repeat misbehaviors by the same students.
- Track students' feedback on the reentry to class after incidents.
- Do a second quarter analysis of misbehavior data.
- Adjust and set new goals for the plan implementation.
- Celebrate successes.

January–March

- Implement adjustments based on wisdom constructed from surveys.
- Do a third quarter analysis of misbehavior data.
- Adjust and set new goals for plan implementation.
- Celebrate successes.

April–June

- Repeat the survey done in January.
- Implement adjustments for the current school year.
- Do a fourth quarter analysis of misbehavior data.
- Adjust and set new goals for plan implementation.
- Celebrate successes.

June–August

- Finalize adjustments for the coming school year.
- Set goals for the coming year regarding decreases in repetitive misbehaviors.

STEP 3. Publicize and make the support for implementation accessible.

A critical component of all educational reform is to provide multiple means of support for implementation that falls heavily on the shoulders of school staff. Too often, I have seen school leaders first present staff with accountability measures as if that will scare them into compliance. This is parallel to threatening students with suspension without offering them help to manage their stress. In both cases, those with authority may get grudging compliance but not the buy-in that predicts long-term growth and stability.

A change from our deeply rooted culture of threats and punishments to one of teaching and restorative discipline will require the support and patience of leadership. Publicizing the investment in support is in the Supports frame and, as important, in the Culture frame, communicating an understanding of the complexity of the staff's work and that the system cares about them.

Methods of support can include:

- Peer coaches and mentors: If you have a Hacking Discipline Committee, the members of that committee are well situated to be coaches and mentors. They will have been early adopters, working through glitches during test runs, providing them with experiences that can build trust with their peers. Create a method for staff to confidentially contact and meet with coaches and peers.
- Office hours with administrators: While many staff will prefer to share their implementation concerns with peer coaches, some will want to talk directly with an administrator. Dedicate office hours solely for conversations about the hacking discipline plan. Staff members and administrators can reference the four steps for sharing concerns from Hack 7. Remember that what can, at first, sound like a complaint is often an intention to improve the plan.
- Invitations to meet with small groups: Staff members often first share their concerns with each other and find common ground. That does not mean they will take the time or energy to share those concerns with leadership. Administrators and Hacking Discipline Committee

members can communicate that they will attend team, grade-level, and department meetings to listen to implementation concerns.

- IT support: Publicize all the ways staff can share concerns with the IT staff. The IT staff can also be among those who welcome invitations to small groups to listen and provide direct instruction.

STEP 4: Anticipate and normalize implementation dips.

The timeline shared earlier includes many opportunities for those in leadership to hear and address staff concerns as the hacking discipline plan is implemented. However, not all staff will read the timeline carefully, nor have confidence that the leaders have the foresight necessary to bring the staff through the dips. Be explicit in staff meetings, coaching sessions, and memos that perfection is not the goal for the staff or the administrators. Reinforce that you will be sticking to the schedule of collecting stories and data and discussing the needed improvements.

These steps and the plan for full implementation correspond with the July–August sample schedule in Hack 1.

OVERCOMING PUSHBACK

All the previous hacks have not required the participation of every staff member, even as the drafts, surveys, and test runs have planted the seeds for full implementation. Now, everyone must participate. Much of the pushbacks explored so far will emerge again and are worth reviewing. Implementation will add a level of anxiety to all prior pushback and reveal new staff reactions and concerns.

The school should not be collecting data about staff implementation. If the leadership has been modeling restorative discipline strategies, sending drafts of various lists and forms, and providing information from test runs throughout the year, most staff will be trying their best to implement the new system. The administration will not be talking to individuals unless there is truly an egregious lack of input; we are looking for trends that require structural fixes.

This is more work that staff is not getting paid for. The wisdom gleaned from research on restorative practices, and hopefully from the test runs in schools, shows that short-term investments in the hacking discipline plan will save time and energy by reducing repeated misbehaviors and incidents. Stronger staff-student relationships will also improve students' focus on their lessons and encourage them to reach out to teachers for academic support—rather than fearing us. That, too, will save time that we now spend on reteaching. The experiences of their peers who have been modeling and implementing test runs should provide assurance to staff that the hacked system is better than the status quo. In the end, teachers will have more time to teach and will spend less time on behavior management.

Students are still misbehaving. The hacking discipline plan promises an increase in student accountability, better relationships with staff, and greater student coping skills. It never promised a cessation of student misbehaviors. I urge you to examine all the structures and routines in your classroom and to identify common stress points that may increase student misbehavior in your setting.

THE HACK IN ACTION

In early August, Anna sent a memo to the Hacking Discipline Committee, once more thanking them for their tremendous work in leading the effort, taking risks in being early adopters, speaking to their peers, and spending time editing drafts of lists and protocols. "Without you," she wrote, "all we had was an idea and a belief that it could change the culture of discipline. Now we have built the future."

Anna invited the committee members to join Maria and her in August as they refine the timeline of the year ahead and double-check that all the documents and systems are ready for full implementation. She wrote, "Please do not change any summer plans to join us. We will be fine. You have done more than your share." Not surprisingly, none of the Hacking Discipline Committee members confirmed that they would show up on the assigned date to complete the timeline.

Anna was at her desk. She heard Maria's steps coming down the hallway when a text message alert pinged on her phone. She was finishing reading it as Maria entered her office. Anna had tears in her eyes.

"We all just got a text from Mr. L's wife," Anna said. "He had a heart attack. He's in the hospital. The medical team says he will be okay, but she says he is going to need to take a leave of absence, maybe for the whole year. It was serious."

Maria took a look at her phone and saw the message. They sat quietly together, stunned, each wiping away tears.

Maria said quietly, "I just keep thinking about him standing up in front of the entire staff in the spring, talking everyone through the work done by the committee and the other staff who tried the protocols. He was so good! He was so clear and calm and confident in the plan for this year. He was right when he said he had to be the one to do that." She cried for a moment.

"Yes, I am holding that memory, too," Anna answered. "After a couple of people pushed back and he answered their concerns, that was it for pushback. He made clear to everyone his support of our plan. We've got our notes from people who identified small details that need attention—but all of them said they wanted us to go forward with the plan." She paused and looked up with a sad smile. "We took a gamble a year ago, asking him to be on the committee. But I think we both knew that beneath his no-nonsense reputation—which he certainly earned—is someone who really cares about the kids and the school. I think by that last staff meeting, he showed he even cares about us."

"I agree," Maria said. "That was the power of the committee. It brought out the best in each of us."

"Well, I am sure it did bring out our best," said Ms. K, the librarian, suddenly stepping into Anna's office, her eyes clearly red from crying. "Mr. L's wife called me first to tell me the news and ask about sending that text—and I was worried you two softies might need a little support. That's why I came down from the library. No way Mr. L would want his heart attack to stop us now."

"You are amazing," said Anna. "Okay, give me a minute to collect myself. Yes, we are here to get work done. Let's take a look at the timeline."

"Oh, I am glad you are all here," said Ms. R, the guidance director, entering Anna's office. She, too, had been crying. "A lot of people are going to have a lot of feelings. I figure this is the place I can be most helpful—and I didn't want to be alone."

There was a knock at the door. "Can I join you?" It was Mr. D, the vocational teacher. "I was down in the shop, fixing my shelves—okay, they needed attention—when I got the text. I'd rather be with you all, working on the timeline."

"Grab a chair, Mr. D," said Maria as she pulled up the draft of the timeline onto the smart board.

Anna interrupted. "Well, now that we have an unofficial committee meeting happening, I need feedback on a different item. Maria and I can do the timeline; it's not that hard. Maria, can you pull up the image of the Lippitt-Knoster matrix? I am concerned that we haven't explored providing more incentives." Once again, she paused to collect herself. "I'm probably not alone in needing to keep absorbing the news. This needs to be a safe place to be sad, and be scared, and carry on, right?" Anna saw everyone nod in quiet agreement, and she continued, "In his own way, Mr. L is both a role model and maybe too much of a role model. He bought into hacking discipline because he saw how our ideas fit into his beliefs. He is an ethical person. All the incentive he needed was to know we were doing the right thing, something that would make the school a better place. Is that enough incentive for the rest of the staff? Is there more we can do?"

REFORMING SCHOOL DISCIPLINE IS ONE OF THE MOST POWERFUL INNOVATIONS TOWARD A CALMER AND MORE COHERENT SCHOOL CULTURE.

For the next half hour, they brainstormed various incentives they could build into the school year and began to integrate those possibilities into the timeline. During that discussion, Mr. P, the physical education teacher, also joined the meeting, unable to wipe away all the tears on his cheeks.

At the same moment, all their phones signaled an incoming text on the Hacking Discipline Committee thread. They looked at each other and then opened their phones. The text was from Mr. L:

> I am writing to tell you I hope to return to work this year. The heart attack may not have been as severe as first thought. We shall see. I have considered retirement the last couple of years; I am prepared to do so. But the work on the committee gave me a new appreciation of my job and our school—but most importantly, of belonging. If the last big action I took in my career was helping get the hacking plan into full implementation, that's not a bad way to end a career. However, I would like to be part of seeing all our efforts bear fruit. So, do not let my heart

attack stop you from working on the timeline today. The future is now."

"That old coot," said Ms. K. "After all these years, he still amazes me. That text is all the incentive I need to keep going today. Let's finish the Lippitt-Knoster matrix and this timeline. We need to have all these parts in place to start the school year."

Reforming school discipline is one of the most powerful innovations toward a calmer and more coherent school culture—touching on all those who enter a school building each day. A successful long-term reform requires that those leading the work be prepared to support the plan through its many hacks, championing the vision and solidifying the infrastructure that will turn a vision into a way of being.

For Administrators:

- What support and resources do you need to develop for your own long-term follow-through on the plan?
- Which data from the early weeks and months of implementation will mean the most to your school?
- Reviewing the Lippitt-Knoster matrix of six critical factors guiding complex change in an organization, where might you need to put more attention?
- What are you learning about implementing change in your school and growing yourself as a leader in the process?

For Staff:

- What data from the first weeks and months of implementation will determine your ongoing buy-in to the plan?
- Who will you turn to when you need support or have concerns about the implementation of the plan?
- From the Lippitt-Knoster matrix of six critical factors guiding complex change in an organization, which factor seems most critical now to your buy-in?

CONCLUSION

HOW YOU CAN GET INVOLVED IN RESTORATIVE DISCIPLINE AT ANY LEVEL

It's tough to make predictions, especially about the future.
— YOGI BERRA, BASEBALL PLAYER AND SPONTANEOUS PHILOSOPHER

RIGHT NOW, IN classrooms and administrative offices in schools across the United States, educators are resisting the culture of punishment and shame to offer skills and restorative practices instead. We are gaining traction, and the data supports our efforts. The research on brain science and learning supports our efforts. The field of trauma-informed practices supports our efforts.

In addition to the positive impact on students, restorative discipline improves the daily experience of educators. We benefit from the physiological response in our bodies when we praise more than redirect or punish students and when we build relationships with students who so desperately need those connections. We gain invaluable professional satisfaction when students develop more coping skills.

We also gain satisfaction in being part of a staff that is practicing restorative discipline. The best schools have a culture that permeates every interaction. Hearing another staff member at lunch sharing a story about de-escalating a tense situation and providing students with ways to restore their good standing motivates all of us to pull in the same direction.

If your school is exploring a restorative discipline practice, let the administration know you want to be part of that effort. If you don't have the time now to be part of the change team, let your administration know you support their efforts. If your grade-level team is struggling with discipline issues, you can begin with those peers to incorporate restorative practices. And if you are only able to implement restorative practices in your own classroom or office, you will still be making a difference in the lives of students and improving your daily experience of working with children.

For administrators, upending the status quo of punishment and shifting into restorative discipline will improve the school culture and unite the staff more than any initiative you can invest in. Pull together a team and begin the journey.

Let's collectively be the generation that builds a status quo of restoration. In that effort, we will get closer to our best visions of teaching and learning and to the feelings of connection to our peers that are at the roots of why we became educators. Let's restore ourselves.

Photo by Steve Friedman

ABOUT THE AUTHOR

Jeffrey Benson has over forty years of experience as a teacher, mentor, and school administrator. His passion is supporting schools to be more successful with more students. He is an internationally known author, and his books include *Hanging In: Strategies for Working with the Students Who Challenge Us Most*; *Ten Steps for Managing Change in Schools*; *Teaching the Whole Teen: Everyday Practices that Promote Success and Resilience in School and Life*; and *Improve Every Lesson Plan with SEL*. He also authored the widely read article "100 Repetitions."

Jeffrey is often hired to lead school change initiatives, facilitating interdisciplinary teams that convert long-standing dilemmas into cutting-edge growth and community-building and creating more inclusive school and classroom cultures. He is a member of the ASCD faculty, is frequently published in education journals, and speaks at conferences on such topics as working with challenging students, integrating SEL into everyday practices, and the science of learning and teaching. His website is JeffreyBenson.org.

ACKNOWLEDGMENTS

HOWARD WOLKE IS the IT guru/teacher (officially the "Digital Learning Coach") in a school where I facilitated a Hacking Discipline Committee. We needed his expertise to develop the internal tracking and communication system regarding discipline. His IT plan bridged the gap between administration and staff, fulfilling a necessary but until-then-idealized part of the vision: reliable communication. He also proved to be an extremely flexible, creative, and thoughtful collaborator with the other committee members, incorporating their feedback to create a system of inputting information and extracting data that does not require his level of technical expertise to use. I reached out to Howard when outlining this book, asking if he could help me frame Hack 9, which is focused on technology. He did more than that: he wrote a first draft. For this book, as with his work on his school's Hacking Discipline Committee, I am indebted to his efforts, without which this book would be incomplete.

I worked for many years in a dual role of teacher and administrator at New Perspectives School in Brookline, Massachusetts, and sadly, the school is no longer operating. Many times, parents of students told me that the staff at the school was magical. I like to think we created an adult culture that unleashed the magic inherent in so many educators. I acknowledge that amazing staff for showing me that supporting and trusting educators makes us all far wiser, if not magical.

I acknowledge all those who worked with me at Germaine Lawrence School. Their relentless compassion for some of the most challenging students in our communities demonstrated the power of hanging in with all young people. Germaine Lawrence was where I first learned how to develop Chill-Out Plans for every student.

I have one superpower: finding and clinging to mentors. All your photos surrounded me as I wrote. I acknowledge that, without your affirmation and guidance, I would have accomplished a fraction of what I have done in my work.

Finally, to Mark Barnes, who never let me slip off his radar in hopes I would write this book way before I even knew this book was within me. Our connections as teachers and writers compelled me to continue sharing stories about inspiring educators and fascinating students. When I said to him, "My stories are what I have," he told me those stories are what I need to tell.

SNEAK PEEK

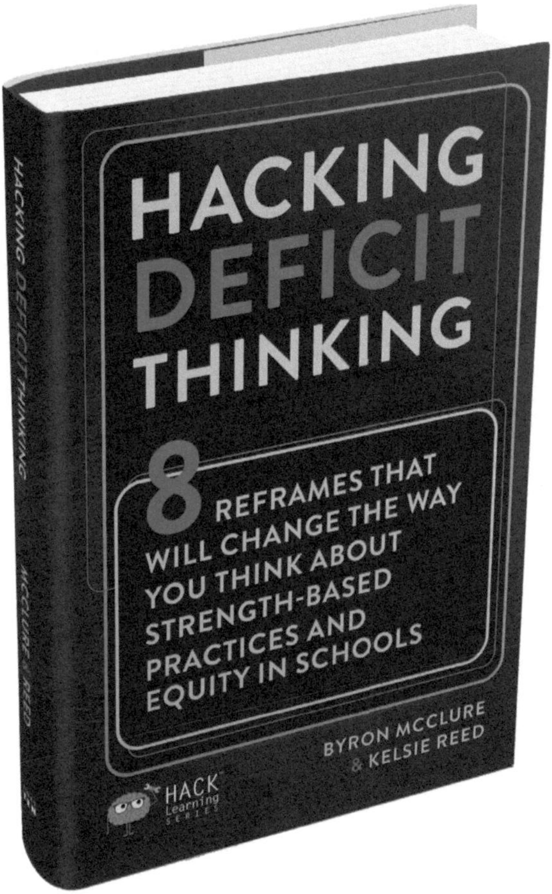
HACKING DEFICIT THINKING
8 REFRAMES THAT WILL CHANGE THE WAY YOU THINK ABOUT STRENGTH-BASED PRACTICES AND EQUITY IN SCHOOLS
BYRON MCCLURE & KELSIE REED
HACK Learning SERIES
HACKING DEFICIT THINKING
MCCLURE & REED

REFRAME

2

OUR PROBLEMS EXIST WITHIN THE SYSTEM

Fix Injustice Not Kids

The education system is so broken by White supremacy, patriarchy, and capitalism, so it's normal for educators to be frustrated or overwhelmed at times because our problems are big and systemic, and a lot of the time, we don't have the resources or authority to address them ... Deficit thinking sneaks in, and instead of naming systemic barriers, we name students or their families as the problem.

— SHANNON WILLIAMSON, DIRECTOR OF A LEARNING RESOURCE CENTER

THE BELIEF:

OUR PROBLEMS EXIST WITHIN THE CHILD

WE ASKED OUR social media followers to share common deficit thinking phrases they hear in their schools regarding students. Have you heard any of these comments?

"They're just REALLY low."

"They're just bad."

"They just don't care as much about education because it's not part of their culture."

"That kid is just lazy."

If you have spent any time inside of a school, you have probably heard similar comments. These comments are rooted in deficit thinking, which centers the blame on the child or their family, community, or culture. This belief falsely blames the student, and it's dangerous for several reasons. For starters, it assumes that a student's potential is fixed and the student can't grow or evolve. Also, it reinforces the idea that a child is inherently inferior. When people make comments like "That child can't learn" or "The apple doesn't fall far from the tree," it's coded language for "The child is intellectually, physically, or emotionally less than their peers." It's a way to attribute weaknesses and deficiencies that become part of who that child is, and no one can do anything about it. The danger in this line of thinking is that it doesn't allow room for growth, teaching, or learning. It sets the standard for low expectations.

The answer? Address the root cause of the problem, not the child. Examine the conditions that are perpetuating the poor outcomes. Students are people, not outcomes, not data points, and not statistics. If students aren't learning or growing as measured by outcomes, then you must examine what's happening from an ecological and systemic approach. Notice and reflect on how systemic inequities have led to injustices in certain communities across generations. Every step we take that helps to address the root cause of systemic inequities will influence change within the educational system.

We've all heard the belief: "Some students thrive while others don't." But focusing on individuals and communities is not the issue. When we prioritize fixing the individual, we risk putting them back into a bad environment. You can see the problem with the approaches in education. Interventions, recommendations, and strategies that we use to "fix kids" never work because then we put them right back into the system that didn't serve them in the first place. This is why certain students, like youth of color and those from high poverty communities, persistently have disproportionate outcomes. Systemic structures cause these inequities. Therefore, we need systemic solutions at the source.

We believe most educators want to make a difference and bring about positive change for their students and school community. The reality is educators work within these complex systems, which often seem toxic and immovable. The topics people often worry or complain about fall into three categories: things we can control, things we cannot control, and those outside of our control and influence. While systemic change is often out of our control, a strength-based approach allows you to focus on areas that are immediately within your sphere of control.

Think about what you have no direct control over. This might include decisions and activities within your political, social, organizational, or personal context; immovable project constraints (such as deadlines or budgets); and other people's attitudes, behaviors, or feelings. Let go of the things outside of your control so you can focus on where you can have the greatest impact. When you can let go of the areas you can't control then you can spend more of your time addressing the areas you have control over.

THE REFRAME:
OUR PROBLEMS EXIST WITHIN THE SYSTEM

Why do you think certain outcomes continue to persist? Seriously, take five minutes and list why you think certain outcomes persist for certain groups of students.

What did you come up with? As you reflect on the source of these issues, notice the source of the problem. Was it because of an inherent problem within the child? Was it because of their culture? *Why?*

Despite decades of research and recommended interventions, certain groups of students continue to have worse outcomes when compared to their peers. *But why?*

Research has documented patterns of disproportionality, as far back as 1968, with students who are minority, high-poverty, and receive special education services. Disproportionality is the over- or under-representation of a group compared to another group in a category. Historically, Black and Latinx students are more likely to be referred and receive special education services than students in other groups.

African American students (aged six to twenty-one) in special education services were twice as likely as their counterparts across all other groups to receive services for intellectual disability (ID) and two times more likely to be identified as having emotional disabilities (ED). In addition, 70 percent of the students who were identified as having an emotional disability were males.

But why?

Data has consistently revealed that racialized youth and students from high poverty communities have historically faced more challenges in school. In addition, research shows a correlation between poverty and academic outcomes. Students in poverty experience less success in school compared with their non-low-income, non-minority counterparts both with and without disabilities.

Behaviorally, youth of color—especially Black males—have historically been referred for disciplinary infractions at disproportionate rates compared to Caucasian students. These negative trends also connect to significantly higher rates of suspensions for youth of color. How many more research studies must exist to show that stressors such as poor nutrition, unsafe living conditions, and high crime rates are more likely to impact youth of color from high poverty communities? We know this. We can predict it, yet these unfair trends continue to persist. *But why?*

Why is it that children who live in persistent poverty are at higher risk for mental illness and in greater need of mental health treatment? Why are youth of color identified as deficient and "at-risk" for these disproportionate outcomes? Despite these persistent and alarming statistics, the academic, behavioral, and mental health needs of youth of color, students from high-poverty communities, and especially African American males are often characterized as being the sole source of their problems. Why is it that students who we can all predict at this point, who are historically under- and overrepresented in the data, are more likely to receive office discipline referrals, be removed from school, and have an increased risk of dropping out of school and entering into the juvenile justice system? *Why?*

We must stop blaming kids and look at solving the problems within the structures of our systems, beliefs, policies, and practices.

The belief that students are to blame and need fixing is erroneous and will continue to perpetuate these outcomes. Instead, it is imperative to examine *the why*. We must also examine the conditions that perpetuate these outcomes for certain students. We must stop blaming kids and look at solving the problems within the structures of our systems, beliefs, policies, and practices, which continue to produce these outcomes for certain groups of students. To understand *the why*, we must get at the groundwater of these problems.

We adopted the metaphor of the groundwater as a helpful way to understand the problem that exists within structures and not kids. Joyce James and Bayard Love first presented this metaphor in 2013. The metaphor aligns with inequity and structural racism.

Many people have difficulty understanding such concepts because of complex terminology, so the metaphor takes a complex concept and makes it easy to understand.

The simple story is about a young child who lives by a massive lake. Each morning, the child would walk past the lake and head to school. One day, the child saw one dead fish floating belly-up. The child thought, "Hmm. What's wrong with that fish?"

(Now, imagine the fish is a student failing in the educational system. We might say, "That child is lazy" or "That kid is bad.")

That same child walked outside the next day and noticed a group of dead fish floating belly-up.

The child said, "Hmm. What's wrong with that group of fish?"

(We might say, "What's wrong with those students from *that* neighborhood?" or "The apple doesn't fall far from the tree.")

The next day, the child walked outside and saw a large number of dead fish floating belly-up. The child finally said, "I wonder what's wrong with the water."

WHAT YOU CAN DO TOMORROW

Most of the water on the planet is not above ground. To understand why the fish aren't thriving, we have to understand there's some sort of contamination. A marine biologist would argue that to fix the contamination, you must identify the source below the surface–in the groundwater. Here are ways you can get to the groundwater of the systemic problems so you can help solve them.

- **Start within your sphere of control.** That means starting with yourself! Raise your self-awareness by identifying and understanding your uniqueness and strengths. To fully understand yourself, aim to recognize the impact and power of your thoughts, choices, conclusions, and assumptions. How does your thinking impact your actions? Create the space to intentionally shift your thinking.

- **Recognize what you can control.** What do you have control over? Regardless of your industry, title, or circumstances, this answer is consistent. Typically, the answer is "only ourselves"—our behaviors and attitudes. As the saying goes, "Your attitude determines your altitude."
- **Recognize what you might be able to influence.** Although we cannot control others, we can influence them. Increase your awareness of your behaviors so you can influence others more effectively. Even a small shift in your mindset or approach can create a far greater impact. Write down two or three areas you might be able to influence.
- **Recognize what you can't influence yet.** Systemic inequities may seem daunting to challenge and influence. Write down one or two areas you can't influence—yet!
- **Look for sources of contamination in your sphere of control.** It's okay to feel overwhelmed and lost as to where to start. Your school is a large, complex system, operating within a myriad of even larger and more complex systems. You can begin by using data (we go into greater detail in Reframe

3) to help you uncover patterns of disproportionality. As an example, a classroom teacher might examine trends in discipline data to see if certain groups of students receive harsher discipline. A psychologist might examine which students are referred for special education services more often than others. A school leader might examine school culture and climate data to identify potential sources of contamination.

A BLUEPRINT FOR FULL IMPLEMENTATION

Follow these steps to develop your skills in avoiding equity detours and taking action.

Step 1: Recognize inequity.

Recognizing inequities is an essential first step because some people might not be aware of systemic inequities and how they impact students, schools, and the broader school community. In education, recognizing inequities might include noticing subtle biases in learning material, social-emotional learning curricula, classroom interactions, classroom policies, and schoolwide practices.

So many of us in the classroom have heard those phrases: "She's a bad student," "She's lazy," or "He doesn't care." It's easy to blame students for our struggles as teachers, but it can also be counterproductive. When you can recognize how inequity is showing up, you can better equip yourself to respond to it.

Tune in to inequity by authentically listening to the needs of people through empathy interviews, which are the cornerstone of design thinking. By entering and understanding another person's thoughts, feelings, and motivations, we can understand their choices and behavioral traits and identify their needs. Once you can understand someone's needs, then you can recognize how inequity might be impacting them from their unique perspective.

Step 2: Respond to inequity.

When you can recognize inequities, you can respond to them. Earlier, we asked why certain outcomes continue to persist. Disproportionate outcomes persist due to a failure to respond to inequities, especially when they are immediate and pervasive.

Responding to inequities is crucial for rooting out contamination at the groundwater level. We showed you a simple and powerful way to respond to inequity. Did you catch it? Earlier, we posed the question—why? Asking why is a simple but powerful tool against inequity. You might notice that Black students are twice as likely to receive an office discipline referral in your school. At your next team meeting, you might simply ask why these disproportionate data exist? As a practice, ask why five times to get to the root cause. Here's an example.

Team leader: Our data shows that Black students in the seventh grade have the highest number of office discipline referrals.

You: But why do they have the highest number of referrals? (why #1)

Team leader: It appears that a group of students, who are most likely Black, are coming into first period and receiving referrals for being tardy.

You: But why is that group of students always late? (why #2)

Team leader: Because they have a longer bus ride compared to other students.

You: Okay, so if they have a longer bus ride, why are they receiving referrals for the bus being late? (why #3)

Team leader: Well, it's just the policy.

You: Why do we have a policy that disproportionately impacts students for an issue that's not their fault? (why #4)

Team leader: We've always had the tardy policy, but we never updated it after the boundaries changed.

You: Why hasn't the policy been updated since the boundary change? (why #5)

Team leader: We never considered it or who it might impact until now. Thank you!

In this example, you can see that the school disciplined a certain group of students due to a policy change. The leaders who made the policy change didn't consider the impact on that group, and it penalized students who had a longer bus ride. You were able to recognize and respond to an inequity immediately, and the team leader took action to immediately redress the inequity.

Step 3: Correct inequity.

Redressing inequities means correcting them. In the prior example, the team leader immediately took action to review the tardy policy, determine who was impacted by it, and create a tardy policy that is more equitable. When you see an inequity, immediately take action to correct it.

Step 4: Actively cultivate equity.

Aim to actively develop your knowledge, skills, and will to apply an equitable lens to everything you do and across every practice and policy in your school. Equity isn't an add-on or task we should force people to perform. Instead, equity is a process of ensuring every student has the access and opportunity to be successful. Systemize these practices by weaving them into the fabric of your school culture and community.

Step 5: Sustain equity.

Commit to doing what's right for children. You can sustain equity by making it a habit to consider who will be impacted positively and negatively by decisions and practices at the classroom, school, and district levels. By reflecting on those who are impacted by decisions, you will constantly look through a lens of doing what's right for children and maximizing the positive impact and minimizing the harm.

Another way to sustain equity is to engage students, staff, parents, and school leaders at key touchpoints. By constantly engaging with all people impacted by your decisions (as well as school or district decisions), you will be aware of potential barriers, instances of harm, and the needs of people. When you engage with people impacted by decisions, you gain valuable insight into what's working and not working. It also allows you to more quickly adapt to their needs and address their concerns. Finally, it opens the door for constant communication and feedback—a powerful tool to support equity.

It won't always be easy, and you may be met with criticism and pushback as you do this worthy work.

MORE FROM
TIMES 10 PUBLICATIONS

Hacking School Discipline

9 Ways to Create a Culture of Empathy and Responsibility Using Restorative Justice

By Nathan Maynard and Brad Weinstein

Reviewers proclaimed this original *Hacking School Discipline* book and *Washington Post* bestseller to be "maybe the most important book a teacher can read, a must for all educators, fabulous, a game-changer!" Teachers and presenters Maynard and Weinstein demonstrate how to eliminate punishment and build a culture of responsible students and independent learners at the classroom level. Twenty-one straight months at #1 on Amazon, *Hacking School Discipline* disrupted education in a big way.

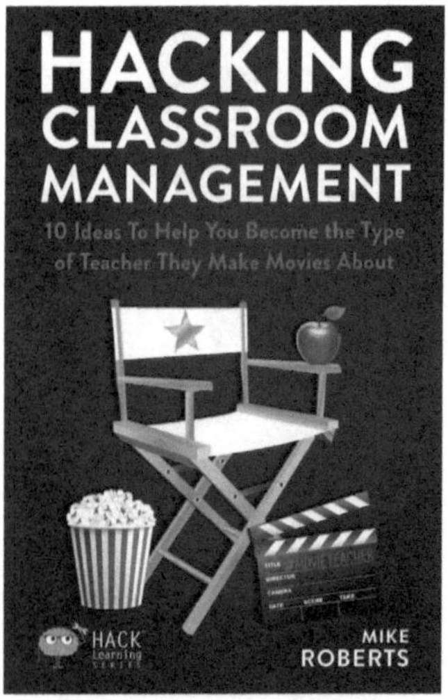

Hacking Classroom Management

10 Ideas to Help You Become the Type of Teacher They Make Movies About

By Mike Roberts

Learn the ten ideas you can use today to create the classroom any great movie teacher would love. Utah English Teacher of the Year and sought-after speaker Mike Roberts brings you quick and easy classroom management Hacks that will make your classroom the place to be for all your students. He shows you how to create an amazing learning environment that makes discipline, rules, and consequences obsolete, no matter if you're a new teacher or a thirty-year veteran teacher.

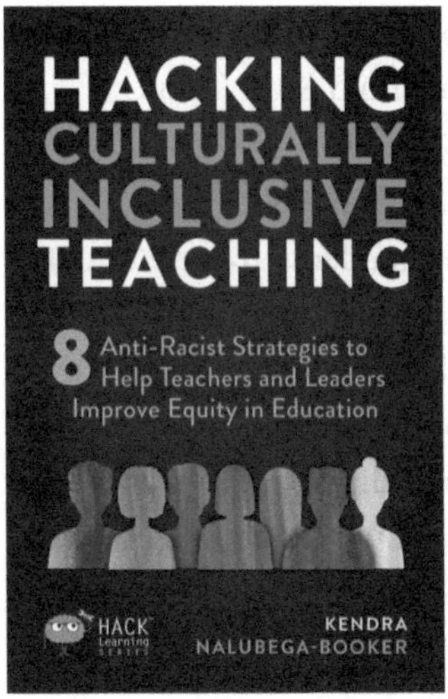

Hacking Culturally Inclusive Teaching

8 Anti-Racist Strategies to Help Teachers and Leaders Improve Equity in Education

By Kendra Nalubega-Booker

Culturally and linguistically diverse students often lack representation and inclusion in the classroom, hindering their academic success. Yet when teachers integrate culturally sustaining practices, they help all students understand our global community and situate themselves within it. Education leader Kendra Nalubega-Booker shows step-by-step strategies and best practices that shine a light on the rich languages and cultures of our students and create equitable learning for all.

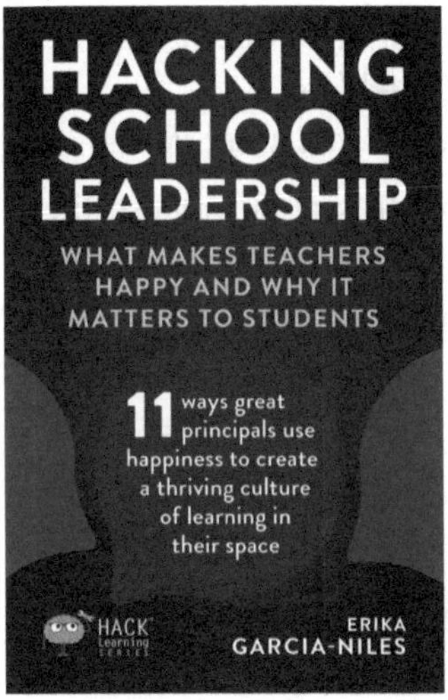

Hacking School Leadership

What Makes Teachers Happy and Why It Matters to Students

11 Ways Great Principals Use Happiness to Create a Thriving Culture of Learning in Their Space

By Erika Garcia-Niles

Hacking School Leadership is not just a book—it's a call to action. It's a call for principals and school leaders like you to champion change, create a culture of support, and prioritize the well-being of teachers. By doing so, you'll not only retain talented educators but also improve student outcomes and foster a vibrant learning community. Erika Garcia-Niles presents a framework of school leadership that is poised to reignite a passion for teaching.

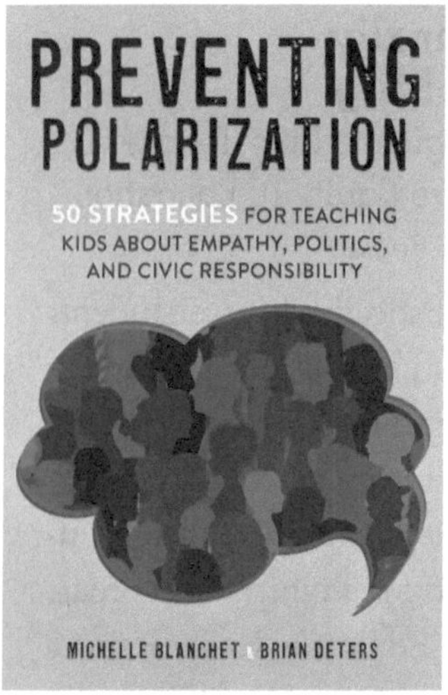

Preventing Polarization

50 Strategies for Teaching Kids About Empathy, Politics, and Civic Responsibility

By Michelle Blanchet and Brian Deters

Education can equip students to care about the world and help them shape their futures. In an era that has become incredibly polarized, we can help our students learn how to come together despite differences. A one-off civics course is not enough to show our students how to become active and engaged citizens, but the strategies in *Preventing Polarization* offer an approach for every teacher to help students break down barriers through activities and role-playing.

Hacking Life After 50

10 Ways to Beat Father Time and Live a Long, Healthy, Joy-Filled Life

By James Alan Sturtevant and Mark Barnes

Father Time is running scared because life after 50 just got hacked! *Hacking Life After 50* shares 10 strategies you can use today to live a long, happy, joy-filled life. After-50s Club members and health and fitness practitioners Sturtevant and Barnes show how to create purpose in life's Act II, build momentum regardless of age, excel in meal planning, reclaim muscle, prolong functional movement, sleep better than ever, and thrive.

RESOURCES FROM TIMES 10 PUBLICATIONS

10Publications.com

Connect with us on social media:

@10Publications
@HackMyLearning
Times 10 Publications on Facebook
Times 10 Publications on LinkedIn

TIMES 10 PUBLICATIONS provides practical solutions that busy people can read today and use tomorrow. We bring you content from experienced researchers and practitioners, and we share it through books, podcasts, webinars, articles, events, and ongoing conversations on social media. Our books and materials help turn practice into action. Stay in touch with us at 10Publications.com and follow our updates @10Publications and #Times10News.

Made in United States
Troutdale, OR
03/28/2024

18763892R00126